Scar Tissue

My fight to survive multiple intense compound traumas in order to break different cycles of toxic generational abuse for the sake of my own next generation

LUCY HENSON

One Printers Way
Altona, MB R0G 0B0
Canada

www.friesenpress.com

First Edition — 2022

ISBN
978-1-03-914300-5 (Hardcover)
978-1-03-914299-2 (Paperback)
978-1-03-914301-2 (eBook)

1. BIOGRAPHY & AUTOBIOGRAPHY, WOMEN

Distributed to the trade by The Ingram Book Company

"*Scar Tissue* is an experience that is raw, and eye opening. A look into a woman's fight to end a cycle of abuse and neglect. You can feel her pain and absolute anger towards her abusers. Eventually her healing, and finally her learning to love herself."

—Vashni Irving, MS/CCC/SLP

"*Scar Tissue* by Lucy Henson is one of the most profound books I have ever read. It is profoundly sad, profoundly tragic, and profoundly disturbing. But it is also profoundly hopeful because it is the story of a very brave and resilient woman who has overcome more trauma than anyone should ever have to suffer in one's life, and not only survived, but found the will to thrive. The issues in this book are deep and dark - racism, generational trauma, sexism, child sexual abuse, narcissistic abuse, domestic violence, poverty and child abuse. But these are stories that need to be shared and I am in awe of Lucy's ability to not only survive these horrors, but to have truly ended the cycle of abuse for her family.

Some stories, no matter how difficult they are to hear, must be told. And we must listen to survivors like Lucy to prevent these tragedies from happening again.

Scar Tissue is a memoir told bravely and boldly by a survivor and is a reminder that while cycles of generational trauma and abuse can be broken, they must be prevented in the first place. Lucy, and every survivor like her, deserves better and if there is one thing you can do, it's to read her story."

—@cant_put_it_down_reviews

"Raw, not pretty, and may be hard to finish if you are looking for a happy ending, Lucy's story is a vivid and rare glimpse into a victim's life, experiencing the worst parts of humanity. If I gave you a small preview of what this woman has endured in 40 short years, it would be easy to believe that I am telling you about multiple women escaping horrible and evil situations from some of the worst parts of the world. But sadly, it is the story of only one woman right here in our backyards. Within the unimaginable and shocking details (which force you to face the dirty truth of generational abuse instead of pretending it doesn't exist) is a story of how the smallest amount of compassion, love, and genuine desire for better can give you the courage to go from victim to survivor."

—Rigoberto A. Murillo, CEO & Chairman,
MW Partners, LLC

Table of Contents

Character Description

As *Scar Tissue* has plenty of key characters, there are some who held a heavy significant position in my life and some less significant to me but important to the story still. Plenty of these people did their part in trying to damage me as a person but still just a couple of good-hearted people along the way was enough to somehow keep me motivated to move forward. Some of these characters are nothing other than evil and responsible for inflicting life-long trauma so please be aware as you continue to read. Allow me to introduce each of them personally.

1. **Sarah.** Sarah is my biological mother. Because of the nature of our relationship, I do not refer to her as my mom but as Sarah. My goal in introducing her the way I do and the way I talk of her early timeline events, is to bring to light how important it is to pay attention to woman with signs of mental illness. Whether it be Posttraumatic stress, whether it be low self-esteem or some postpartum depression. Whatever the case may be, a toxic woman/parent can often be the tip of a downward spiral for children.
2. **Lucy.** I myself am first born child to Sarah and I am author of this story – (Fathered by Robin Hardridge)
3. **Ralph.** Ralph is second born child to Sarah and brother to Lucy. As you read further you will understand that it is with this brother Ralph that I have the closest bond.

We are 14 months apart in age and have been through the thick of life together. – (Fathered by Lupe)

4. **Sandra.** Sandra is the third child born to Sarah and youngest sister to Lucy. Sandra and I had a fairly close relationship while we were children but after forms of abuse happened to us both our bond lessened. My fortitude took me one way her loyalty to her parents kept her closer – (Fathered by KD)

5. **DJ.** DJ is fourth born child to Sarah and youngest brother to Lucy. DJ has a heart of gold – (Fathered by KD)

6. **Robin Hardridge.** You will learn later in this story how I come to find out the name of my biological father who at the time of my birth was no longer in contact with Sarah. The two of them had a "one night stand" and as a result of that she became pregnant. She did not make him aware of the pregnancy being that he already had a family, and she was newly married as well.

7. **Lupe.** Lupe is the biological father to my closest sibling Ralph. Much like myself, Ralph did not grow up with his father and was not able to form his own bond. Lupe not being a citizen of the United States was also not in contact with Sarah at the time of Ralphs birth.

8. **Robert H.** Robert is first husband to Sarah as well as the man she tried to get me to accept as my natural father. As you read on you will see that Robert had less interest in being a father figure.

9. **Leonardo.** Even though Leonardo has a small place in these pages he still holds a significant spot. This relationship will be Sarah's second husband, a man she allegedly marries for convenience and at the end suffered a brutal

beating at his hands. After the loss of what would have been Sarah's third child, Leonardo was out of the scene.

10. **KD.** KD is third husband to Sarah as well as her fifth marriage. He married Sarah while I was a toddler and was an abusive stepparent to me for roughly 8 years. He is the father of my two younger siblings Sandra and DJ. KD played a key role in my mental, physical and emotional abuse as a child. The two of them divorced for several years then married again later in the years.
11. **Alvie Wilson.** Alvie was my first sexual abuser while I was still a toddler.
12. **Elaine Wilson.** Elaine was Sarah's best friend during my childhood as well as older sister to Alvie Wilson which how I was introduced to my first child sex predator.
13. **Yolanda.** Yolanda was a friend to Sarah during my early childhood.
14. **James Wallace.** James was a sex abuser responsible for taking my virginity while I was still a child. James was also responsible for my first pregnancy when I was just 14 years old that ended in a miscarriage in my first trimester.
15. **Dan.** Dan was a boyfriend to Sarah after her divorce from KD. He was an abuser responsible for introducing me to alcohol as a child in order to take advantage of my body.
16. **Mel.** Mel was another boyfriend to Sarah after her divorce from KD. He introduced me to smoking marijuana and was also a rapist to me for a period as a teen. Mel had a deep negative mental impact on me. He manipulated what I thought the concept of love was

while sexually used my body and influenced my mind as well.

17. **Brenda** was girlfriend to Mel before he became intensely involved with our family.
18. **Penny** was daughter to Brenda as well as a negative influence for in my teen years.
19. **Johnnie.** Johnnie was sex abuser that whom when I was 14 Sarah allowed to have a sexual relationship with me. By a plan orchestrated by Sarah, Johnnie lived in my room and sexually assaulted me daily for several months. He too had deep negative impact on my impression of love.
20. **Paul Archer.** Paul not a boyfriend but husband number four to Sarah and abusive stepparent to me and siblings. The importance of Paul in this story is that if you are a person who doesn't want children then don't marry into a family with children. Sarah's marriage to Paul was short lived but wasn't without verbal and physical abuse along with family conflict with added animosity.
21. **Kirby Archer.** Kirby was younger brother to Paul Archer and our step uncle during the marriage between Paul and Sarah. Although he was now an uncle, he was also a sex predator, so I was not spared from him either.
22. **Tonya.** Tonya was younger sister to Shannon Beasley and introduced to two of us initially.
23. **Shannon Beasley.** With me being 16 and him being barely 18, Shannon became my first husband, the father to my first child and my first domestically violent relationship.

24. **Wilene/Willy B.** Wilene is mother to Shannon and the first woman I felt a close connection to. She at times sacrificed her own being to protect me from physical abuse.

25. **Mike Walker.** Mike is the father to my two youngest children. I did stepparent his toddler son for 10 years and him the same for my toddler son. Mike was my second abusive relationship and ultimately the reason for my suicide attempt. Narcissistic persons are suffering from a disorder of their own and cannot be "fixed if you love them enough." Mike too played a heavy part in my psychological damage with his verbal mental emotional and physical abuse to me.

26. **Cindi.** Cindi. Although her name sounds the same, her name is spelled with an I whereas Mike's mother Cindy is spelled with a y. Although she was just a teen at the time, she had a very manipulative and vindictive personality. Cindi and Mike's "personal relationship" broke my spirit as it was flaunted so heavily in front of me.

27. **Crickett.** Crickett is mother to Mike Walker's son Mike Jr and the boy I step parented for 10 years.

28. **Bubba.** Bubba is younger brother to Mike Walker

29. **Cindy Walker.** Mother to Mike Walker and grandmother to my 2 youngest children.

30. **Sonny Sr.** Sonny Sr. is father to Mike Walker and grandfather to my 2 youngest children

31. **Billy.** Billy was younger boyfriend to Cindy and the one who tried desperately to intervene when Mike was physically beating me on the kitchen floor.

32. **Mandi Jordan.** Close friend and councilor at the time I attempted a suicide by overdose.

33. **Staci.** Current therapist.
34. **Tara.** Close friend and church family
35. **Poppa and Jenni.** Close friends considered family. As a single parent of 3 children, they had seen how much I needed support and quickly became that for myself and my children.
36. **William Henson.** Will is the light at the end of my tunnel I told you about in introduction. After all the years of suffering by many different hands God sent me someone to walk with me. I am no longer alone, neglected or unloved. It isn't easy for him to understand me at times. It isn't easy for him to handle the emotional baggage that comes with me either, but he is my God sent support and he comes with everlasting love.

Introduction

Hello to you, reader. I hope your days are good and happy. My name is Lucy, and the story you are about to read belongs to me. I must say that it's not a beautiful story by any means, and honestly, it doesn't really get happy until the end. Nonetheless, it's very much a true story. At times, the situations are very crude and vulgar, and most often embarrassing as well as traumatic, to say the least, so please beware. Not to worry though. I do have a smile of a sort as I sit and tell you today that there is a light at the end of my dark, toxic tunnel—a light and a love that I can finally be thankful for. I can say that I made it. I was able to find some peace.

It isn't easy for me to allow people to know my story. These pages are filled with a shame that weighed me down with its heavy burden for countless years, but ultimately, I tell it to you for a reason: my own daughter. I could never in my lifetime allow the things that plague this story to happen to her. I see the close bond and happy relationships she has with her peers and can't imagine these sorts of things happening to the people she loves, or how much her heart would be broken if they did. The trauma in this story should never happen to anyone, child or adult, in my own family, in yours . . . not in anyone's.

So, I will be open and share these intimate pages in the hopes that it will enable you to see more clearly the cycles of neglect, abuse, and everything else these sorts of toxic environments generate, through a different perspective, and allow you to notice things you didn't before so perhaps you will be able to make a positive difference in the life of someone else. Maybe it will even allow you to see if (perhaps) you could use a change within yourself.

The responsibility to protect our children at any cost, and always strive to be better people, is ours.

Thank you in advance and good day to you.

—Lucy

Chapter 1

Where in the fuck did she even find this guy?

KD was our stepfather for a number of years as children. He tortured us. For as long as I can remember him being in our lives, he inflicted nothing but pain and fear. I can still smell his nasty, disgusting breath and the spit that would fly into my face when he'd go off on us. If he thought that we weren't "listening to him," he'd press his nose against our child noses and scream as loudly as he could to ensure that he had our attention. He frightened the life out me. As if that wasn't enough to scare the living shit out of us, he'd then turn us sideways and scream into our ears at the top of his fucking voice, so he knew we could hear him when he talked to us. It was terror: the sound of his voice screaming into my ears that me and my siblings were "so fucking stupid and hard of hearing" that maybe we needed hearing aids.

For some time during our childhood, we lived at 537 North 10th Street in Ponca City, across from the pet shop. So much abuse from him happened in that house. Like the "Hummer." Let me explain:

In Ponca City at the time—the late eighties and early nineties—the Wednesday paper was the thickest paper of the week.

I know this because my brother Ralph and I used to help a neighborhood girl and her little brother roll newspapers for their paper-route delivery. Back then, a person would get their daily paper delivered to the front door by some kid on a bike who was trying to make a couple of extra bucks.

The Wednesday paper was the thickest because it contained all the ads for the week, all the grocery coupons, the funny pages, and a paper TV Guide, which was flat like the paper but in a book form. It had all show listings, with their airing times and channels, for the entire week through weekend. That TV Guide just added to the thickness. KD would take that Wednesday paper and roll it and roll it again, as tight as he could get it. Then he'd wrap that rolled-up newspaper with gray duct tape, so that when it was finished, his product looked like a steel bar and felt like one to our child bodies. "Hummer" was the name he gave those faux metal bars.

Before I go any further, let me give you the larger picture here: Sarah (my mother) and KD married when I was three or four years old, and Ralph was two or three. They divorced when we were roughly nine and ten years old. So, this sick fuck was with us for what almost anyone would agree are both fragile and formative years for children, when they are supposed to have active and developing imaginations. They are the years when hugging and reassurance is key to positive development; years when bonding and support are crucially important. We didn't have hugging. We didn't have happy. We didn't have nurturing or bonding. No. We had Sarah (our mentally unstable mother) and KD, a sadistic stepdad who had no business raising anyone's children.

Getting back to the story, getting hit with the hummer was no joke. To this day, KD actively jokes about how he could sling that thing at us from any place in the house and knock us down, which—while a disgusting thing to brag about—is the absolute truth. One hundred percent. As long as he had the hummer sitting next to his overflowing pile of cigarette butts, which took up space on the small metal food tray beside his chair, he didn't need to get up to hand down punishment. Not to say that he wouldn't, but if he didn't want to get up, he could sling that imitation metal bar and bruise our bodies from across the room. Whether or not he was able to knock us down depended on how hard he slung it. In the late eighties and early nineties, I guess the school system didn't pay much attention to bruised children. Maybe the most humiliating part of his use of the hummer wasn't that we were knocked down but rather that we were then forced to fetch his weapon of destruction and return it to its rightful position on the tray table.

I have to say that when KD used the hummer, or spanked us with the "paddle" (which was just a flat board really), or whipped us with his belt, it was never about punishing us for anything real. It was just an opportunity for him to take out his aggressions. If work upset him, we were getting a beating. If Sarah upset him, we were getting a beating. If we acted as normal kids do and displayed any kind of rambunctiousness, you can be sure he saw good reason to either throw or swing something at us. Each time he threw or swung a weapon at us, I felt his anger and disconnect from us as a "parent." His dislike of us was always evident, even in the way that he spoke to us in normal day-to-day life. So, you can be damn sure that when he had a chance to swing his paddle or his belt, or sling that damned hummer, he always had a full arsenal of degrading words for "his" young children at the ready.

One time, KD had my brother bent over his lap, giving him a spanking with the paddle. He held Ralph down and hit him so hard that Ralph screamed out in pain. When I yelled for KD to stop because he was hurting my brother, KD looked me in the face, wrapped his legs around Ralph like a pretzel, screamed at me, "How much do you like it now?" and then proceeded to hit him even harder. In his sick sadistic way, he knew that he could hurt both of us by just getting one of us. He knew that hitting Ralph harder would shut me down. He wanted us to fear him. No love. Just fear. No mercy. And no help from "Mom."

I don't remember Sarah ever stepping in. She claims now that she and him had plenty of fights over us, and that she defended us in private. I find that claim extremely laughable. If I'm in a position where I feel my children need defending (whether or not they *actually* do), I start roaring like a mother lioness—as my husband is quick to tell everyone. Any mom who is truly interested in defending her children will make sure her voice is heard loud and clear. And if that doesn't do the trick, then just like a mother lion, she will do whatever it takes to protect them, even if that means killing their attacker at the risk of being killed herself. A real mother protects her young . . . unless that mother is Sarah. I never heard her say a word to protect us or saw her lift a finger in our defense. Not as a child and not any time since. Ralph and I were on our own—as were our two younger siblings, DJ and Sandra, who would be born to KD and Sarah over the next few years. We did what we could to protect each other, though it was never enough.

I can honestly say that every waking moment with KD was a nightmare that I could feel like a sharp rock in the pit of my stomach. I'm forty years old as I write this, and I cannot recall one single true, loving moment that KD shared with us. When I was a small girl, I was in such fear of him that now all I can remember of him is anger and rage. Was he ever happy to be our dad? I can't answer my own question, because if there ever was such a moment—one where he was proud or looked at us with fondness—he never let us see it. He certainly never expressed it.

At my wedding to Will, I absolutely did *not* want KD there. Unfortunately, I hadn't gotten to a point in my life, or my mind, where I was able to muster up the courage to tell him to stay away from me. I regret that so much. Though I did not let him walk me down the aisle, I hate that I still felt obligated to allow him in my life . . . and my wedding photos. But I did. I played my part, and when it came time for KD and me to take a photo together, I faked my way through it.

Do any of you know how that feels? To force yourself to pretend everything is normal and look "happy" while plagued with so much animosity? I hate KD. I feel absolutely zero love for him. I certainly don't like him. Despite knowing him all my life, I feel no bond. And I can't summon even an ounce of compassion for him, though one would assume someone or something shaped him into the monster he became. Despite how far I've come, in so many ways, there's only hate. I know that's a strong word, but I mean it each and every time I say it. I hated that son of a bitch as a child, and I hated him just as much on my wedding day. I hate that he was in my pictures, and I hate that I forced myself not to vomit when he put his grotesque arm around me and ruined my photos, pretending that he should even be there at all. But he was. I went along with it. I was determined not to ruin the day that would unite me with Will.

* * *

As bad as KD was, I still find it impossible to understand why he married Sarah in the first place. What did he find attractive about her? When Sarah and KD married, he already had one marriage under his belt. A marriage and a family. A wife and a son. We met him later in life, but there was never any connection really, as he was never around while we were growing up. It wasn't hard to imagine why KD and his first family had gone their separate ways, freeing him up to find us. The next targets for his toxicity.

In terms of Sarah choosing him, I was told that KD had been working for a traveling carnival that had come through town. They met, hooked up, and the rest is history. I guess she started working for the carnival too, because at one point, Sarah told us about one time when she had been driving one of the carnival vans and had fallen asleep behind the wheel, which resulted in an accident and a visit to the emergency room. There she received several stitches in her head. I've often wondered if the accident also caused some dental damage, as she's had bad teeth for as long as I can remember. Of course, it's possible that issue started before she ever met KD. I wouldn't know, as I was so young when they got together. But from what little I recall, and what I've managed to piece together over the years, Sarah did a lot of living before she met him.

Right before she met KD, but after Ralph and I had been born, Sarah had gotten involved with a Hispanic man named Leonardo—who was in the States illegally—and married him. I'm positive I remember her talking about marrying this man just because it would help him gain citizenship. I don't know how that process worked in the eighties, but that's what she said. She became pregnant from this marriage, but when she was already far enough along that it could be determined she was carrying a boy, the pregnancy was terminated by a vicious beating at the hands of the man she'd married "just because."

I have to wonder where Ralph and I were while Sarah was with this man. We were only babies at the time. Did he have access to us? Was he our stepdad? Did we witness this brutal beating that killed our sibling? The timeline, as I understand it, says that at twenty years old, even before marrying this violent offender and having a miscarriage, Sarah had already married and divorced another man, Robert H., whom I will get to a bit later.

As an adult woman now, I have to wonder how this sort of mental/emotional trauma might affect a normal person—although even at that point in her life, I doubt she could have been classified as "normal." As young as she was, she already had a baby and a toddler, was on her second marriage, and had just been beaten into a miscarriage.

Though Ralph and I are only fourteen months apart in age, we do not share the same father. Sarah birthed me four months after she turned eighteen, and I spent many years uncertain who my biological father actually was (which I will also get to later).

Ralph's father was a man named Lupe—another Hispanic man who was in the country illegally. I was born in June of 1980 and Ralph in August of 1981. Did Sarah and Lupe date? Did they just hook up once and get pregnant, or did she actually make an attempt to give Ralph a real father? Either way, it wasn't good for Sarah, with two kids now and a third child now deceased. At this point, was she just tired of getting her ass kicked and decided when she met KD that he would be a better option?

In any case, at approximately two and three years old, without us having had the opportunity to have a relationship with our own fathers, Sarah brought us some sorry fuck she'd met at the traveling carnival instead. Nothing will ever make me understand how she could've possibly looked at this guy and thought, *Yep, this is the guy who will love my children.* Was that scrawny piece of garbage really the dad we'd been missing? I sometimes wish I could go back in time and wring her neck.

Sarah, just one fucking time . . . could you please make a good decision for us?

I don't know much about Sarah's parents at all. I don't remember her ever telling stories about our grandparents, though she once did grab me by the arm and comment on how I had my grandfather's elbows, whatever that meant. Other than that, it's a completely blank history. She never brought out a photo album and shared stories of the past, and she only spoke of her parents to share the story of their deaths.

Their names were Ralph and Lucille—yes, she did name us after those same people she never spoke of—and I do have a black and white photo of the two of them together. I took it from Sarah because I knew she'd never just give it to me. Along with it, I have two other photos that allow me at least a glimpse of my grandparents, from which I have formed my own impressions of them. One of those photos is of Sarah, Grandfather Ralph, and me as a new infant. I couldn't have been more than a few weeks old. She is eighteen in the picture, and he is an old gray-haired man that raised five daughters and no sons. Sarah was the youngest of the five.

I only remember ever seeing two pictures of my grandmother. There must have been pictures of my grandparents in my aunts' homes, but I was young and pictures on the walls weren't something I paid attention to. There is the one black and white photo of my grandparents together, and the other is a family picture of my grandparents with all five of their daughters. It was taken when Sarah was around ten years old, sixteen years younger than the next youngest child. Yikes! My poor grandparents. I can't imagine raising four daughters into adulthood and then having one last daughter. I can't help thinking that, after a woman raises four daughters, her energy and patience might be a running little thin by the time the last one arrives. I guess my question would be whether or not Ralph and Lucille gave Sarah the upbringing that the other girls received. Did she get the same parenting attention? Or any parenting at all? The same support, attention, punishment, and everyday family life that the others got to experience? Just how different was it for her being basically an only child?

I imagine that, by the time Sarah was born in 1962, the first two or three daughters would have already been out of the house. So, when "Dad" was at work, that would have left a sixteen-year-old and an infant at home with their mother, who had already done her fair share of raising children, to say the least.

You're not done yet though, Lucille, because you made another baby...

* * *

Was Sarah's primary care left to a sixteen-year-old on the verge of spreading her own wings or did Lucille truly raise her last daughter? Of course, I'll never know the answer to any of my questions, because (again) Sarah didn't talk about her parents. She really didn't share stories about her and her sisters either, though with them all being so much older, I don't know what kind of stories she would have had with them.

So, was Lucille a good mom to Sarah, even though then she was a much older mother, or did Ralph take the reins? Was it a normal family environment? Who knows? I didn't give it any mind when I was a kid—Sarah's lack of acknowledgment for her parents, I mean. But now that I've lived some of my own life, it has made me stop and ask myself, *What kind of relationship ends with a daughter not talking about her parents even after their deaths?*

By the time the photo of Grandfather Ralph, myself as an infant, and Sarah was taken, in July or August of 1980, my grandmother Lucille had already passed. Before I was born, she was killed in an automobile accident on July 4, 1979, the day Sarah was set to be married for the first time, to Robert H.

Sarah was seventeen (and five months), and Robert H. was twenty-one, and their wedding was all set to happen when someone received a phone call and was told that there had been an accident involving both of Sarah's parents, an aunt, and a young cousin. The group had been headed to the wedding when (perhaps) the driver swerved, lost control of the vehicle, and it rolled over several times. On the day she was set to marry Robert H., Sarah lost both her mother and an aunt in this accident.

There are some details I don't know. I don't know if Sarah ever laid eyes on her dead mother that day. I do recall her saying that she'd witnessed nurses pulling glass from her father, but he was still alive. I don't know her actions immediately following the accident. I don't know how long it took her to get to the hospital after the initial phone call. I don't know a ton of details, because of course, this was all before I was born, and I've had to piece things together.

Let me tell you what I do know for a fact. On that exact day, July 4, 1979, the same day that seventeen-year-old Sarah experienced the death of her mother, saw her father bloody and full of glass shards in a hospital bed, and understood that she had also lost an aunt in the rollover accident that had killed her mom . . . she went through with her marriage to Robert H. On the exact same day.

I have questions about these actions.

To me (and I kind of feel to most people), this doesn't seem like a normal response to the happenings of the day. Going ahead and getting married is not a normal thing to do in response to what most of us would consider the most tragic event of a person's life. So, why did Sarah do it? Was it shock? Did she just carry on that day because she honestly lost her damn mind? Was that the day that triggered a lifelong series of shit decisions? Could that be it?

Or did she do it because she already had detachment issues with her mother before that day, which later manifested once again with her children? The day Lucille was killed, did it matter so little to Sarah that she just didn't allow it to interrupt her day? Maybe. But what about everyone else in the vehicle? Did none of them matter to her either? Has Sarah always been a selfish bitch, or was that the day that she checked out mentally? Was she pressured by someone to continue with the wedding? Was there anyone around her that day to give her any kind of support or guidance? Sarah would never answer such questions. Honestly, I'm surprised she told us as much as she did.

In any case, I don't know if her undiagnosed mental illness started that day or some time before. Nobody will ever know that except for Sarah. What she has been willing to share about that day is that she was, in fact, drunk when she said, "I do."

I can be pretty certain that she didn't marry Robert H. that day because of pregnancy. I did the math, and unless she birthed me at forty-four weeks pregnant, then that isn't a possibility. Of course, freaky things do happen all the time, but since I weighed only six pounds at birth, and she delivered me healthy, I'm sticking with "not pregnant."

There's a bit of controversy surrounding my paternity. Do your best to follow along: Robert H. marries Sarah on July 4, 1979. June 21, 1980, Sarah births me, her first-born child. Ralph is born fourteen months later in August of 1981, fathered by a different man: Lupe. Sarah's first marriage didn't last long. The math says that she hooked up with Lupe when I was twelve months old.

So, she had a husband. Then she didn't. She had a sex buddy (at least) in Lupe and gets pregnant with Ralph. My assumption is that there was no long-term dating between them, because Lupe was at constant risk of being deported. I'm sure that he did, in fact, end up back in his home country.

I wonder who was watching me while Sarah was out getting pregnant again. Did she get a sitter while she was out hooking up instead of at home with her infant daughter? Again, who knows? Only Sarah.

So, baby Ralph is born in 1981, and by the time Sarah is nineteen years old, she is a high-school dropout with two kids and two baby daddies. That's when she meets Leonardo. Remember him? So, how long after having a baby with Lupe did she move on to Leonardo, unknowingly signing up not only for a marriage of convenience but a brutal beating and the loss of her third child as well? Was it this beating and the death of her child that damaged her to the extent that she completely detached from her responsibility to Ralph and me?

All this was before she turned twenty-one, in 1984, shortly after which I would turn four. I don't specifically remember KD being in the picture at all during any of that time, but they say that he was. If that's the case though, where was he?

Chapter 2

I don't remember much from before KD's time. For example, I remember KD's silver mobile home, which Sarah took us to visit, but I don't remember them getting married. But one memory that remains all too clear, unfortunately, involves the brother of Elaine Wilson, who was Sarah's best friend. His name was Alvie.

Not everyone knows this, but I've had to bare my soul in therapy to keep from killing myself over my memories of Alvie alone, aside from every other trauma I would eventually have to heal from. Between my therapist Staci and I, we have concluded that my very first memory was formed around the age of three or four.

I wish I could tell you who met who first, or who introduced one asshole to the other, but I guess none of that really matters. The Wilson family was around for most of my childhood. Sarah and Elaine Wilson were best friends, like I said. I can still smell that Wilson house. I would never in my lifetime leave my own child, nor even any of my animals, in that house for any amount of time. I don't know that there's a word to accurately describe the Wilson house. "Vile" maybe. The house and property were so disgusting and full of trash that a person could literally stand out in the yard and smell the putrid odor seeping out of that house.

It's wood was so rotten that the structure was barely holding together. It had an unstable front porch, with slats of wood missing in various spots, and we'd have to be careful not to fall through. The grass in the yard was worn nonexistent by their dogs, which were always chained to the trees and left largely unfed and totally unloved and were never cleaned up after. The yard was blanketed in dog feces, torn-up toys, and trash.

The moment you walked into the Wilson house, you were hit was by the smell of various piles of unpleasantness. One might wonder: *What in the fuck could be making such a foul odor?* But it would quickly become clear. Stained bed sheets hung in the windows where curtains should be, garbage was piled on top of garbage, and under all that garbage were piles of dog and cat feces and puddles of urine, left to dry on the hardwood to become permanent additions to the décor, their odors permeating the air. Dirty laundry was piled all around—not in baskets but in actual piles on the floor for the cats and dogs to use as a litter box. I'm sure the walls had once been some shade of white, but because nothing was ever cleaned or washed, the walls had turned into canvases for dirty handprints, spills, and splashes. Add the cigarette smoke of people unconcerned with the risks of secondhand smoke to the lungs of children, and after time, the walls had turned a yellowish brown. The bedrooms were decorated with sheetless mattresses laid down on a urine-stained floor. Nobody had a normal bedframe. If they were lucky, they might have had a box spring, but one with the springs busted and poking through the material. It didn't matter the condition or shape of the mattresses though, because they too were soaked through with piss from both the animals and the kids who were forced to sleep there. Trash and laundry was strewn throughout the entire house. I simply cannot explain to you the layers of filth and dirt.

To make it worse, we were never at the Wilson house when the sewers weren't backed up into the bathroom, leaving piss-soaked toilet paper stuck to the hardwood floor. Not surprisingly, there was mold throughout the bathroom and in the kitchen area as well, which was continually piled to the ceiling with trash and dirty dishes (or so it seemed). Do any of you know what cockroaches smell like? Did you even know that they have an odor? I do. There were wall-to-wall roaches in the Wilson house—roaches so bad that they infested every single hole, crack, crevice, and corner. It was common to see maggots in that kitchen as well, in the overflowing garbage can and floor. The scene never changed. That was their world.

Elaine lived there with her partner Paul, though he wasn't always there. They had three children: Rick, Bee, and Randy. They were about the same age as Ralph and me. There wasn't a time when they didn't have head lice, and you could clearly see the black bugs in their fire-red hair.

Yes, this was Sarah's best friend. We spent so much time there as kids, having absolutely no choice at all but to follow Sarah around and be surrounded by the same filth that she chose for herself. We were forced to be there. Sarah was perfectly happy living like scum herself, so of course, she attracted scum-of-the earth people. That was her crowd, so sadly, it was our crowd too.

Elaine Wilson was a large woman and lacked any kind of awareness of proper grooming or hygiene and always smelled just like the inside of her house. She was perfectly fine walking around the house I just described in her bare feet. Paul was exactly the sort of mate you'd imagine her having: an emaciated man with big, bushy black hair, Coke-bottle glasses, and no sense of self-worth for himself or his family. He worked at a garage and was constantly dirty, which he seemed fine with. The older two kids had freckles and fiery red hair to go with their fair skin, and the youngest had black hair. For some time, for as far back as I can remember, Elaine and Sarah tried to convince Randy and me that we were brother and sister, and that the both of us belonged to Robert H. I think Randy may have believed it for a short time, but I was always skeptical of anything Sarah had to say. They did what they could to get us to process this lie, purposefully trying to confuse us and never able to provide proof of any siblingship between myself and Randy.

As a child, I remember watching adult situations in that house, aware that though fewer people were allowed in and out of that house than seemed normal, those that were there were often inappropriate. Dirty talking was a thing then, and the adults didn't do anything to hide it, showing no modesty at all in front of us. Sexual talk was very open and loud. They used to play this game over the phone called "The Breather." It was played when someone would call one of the women in the Wilson house on the landline and then go on to breathe heavily—obscenely. The woman who'd answered would respond by talking dirty back into the phone. It was disturbing to watch and disturbing that they—meaning Sarah, Elaine, or other women whom I'm sure were female relatives of Elaine—allowed me and their own daughters to be exposed to (and influenced by) this sexual behavior at our young ages. It was disturbing that these same women also taught us how to write dirty letters to adult men. We'd each pick a guy to write about, then go on to describe how we wanted to give them oral sex, how much we wanted to be touched in return, and so on.

Yep. As children, we were taught how to write out pornographic letters to adult men, detailing specific sexual actions meant to be between two consenting adults, not one adult and a kid—not even a teenaged boy and a kid, which was also common. After our letters were written out, we'd then take turns reading those letters out loud, laughing ("Ewwww!"), and making fun of each other. Then we'd just throw them away. Eventually (for me anyways), all the shit in those letters—plus so much more than I could have imagined—played out in real life.

Pornography was so common in the Wilson house that rumor had it that two of the Wilson kids were doing sexual activities with each other. The fucking adults did that to them, warping their minds so much that they became abnormal, and what sickens me the most is that none of those adults will face any punishment for that—for ruining children. It's so very wrong.

* * *

People always ask kids, "What do you want to be when you grow up?" Most of the kids around me would have an immediate answer, but I never did. I never had an answer to that question, and to this day, I'm still not sure that I do. As an adult, I understand that those kids often had a quick answer because they had some kind of role model they looked up to, or an imagination so active that they could picture themselves as a hero of some kind. Maybe they even had someone in their young lives who let them know their great potential in this life, acting as a cheerleader of sorts.

When someone would ask me that question, I'd try so hard to come up with something. Anything at all. Any answer that sounded "neat" or "cool." Something logical maybe. But most of the time, I just didn't have a lie ready. I'd draw a blank. So, my most common answer was simply, "I don't know." Then I'd put my head down, where it felt most comfortable. I can't imagine the look I wore on my face in those moments, as each time, my mind would wander back to the same place and time. Every time, without saying a word about what was on my mind. I could never figure out why I didn't have an answer for that question.

Every kid wants to be something, if only for a short moment. Not me.

If I encounter a child with a blank expression now, I start a conversation with them—nervously, because you never really know what's behind that sort of blank stare unless they are willing to come right out with it. Lots of kids carry on and on about what might be happening in their lives, and some won't tell a soul. If someone would have asked me what I was thinking about, rather than what I wanted to be when I grew up, I might have said, "Alvie, Elaine Wilson's kid brother." Elaine Wilson had two or three brothers, but he was the youngest, and he is my very first memory. Not Sarah. Not my father. Not a day at the park, a funny story, or something with my siblings. My first memory is of Alvie.

I was small. I was sitting in the backseat of a car when Alvie took me out of that back seat. We were parked at a Sonic drive-up. Alvie took me into an outside bathroom on the side of the building, unzipped his pants, pulled out his entire penis, and put it into my mouth. To this day, I remember Alvie's hands on my face. I clearly remember biting him too, because I guess that's what I thought I should do. That's what a toddler does when something goes in their mouth. They bite. That is what I did. Alvie smacked me on top of my head. I don't believe I cried. He then took me back around and put me back into the backseat of that car.

I still remember Alvie putting himself in my mouth like it happened yesterday. Like it happened twenty minutes ago. I don't remember if I thought or felt anything at that moment in time other than that it was just something that happened. I don't remember saying a word.

I don't know where Sarah was. I don't know where KD was. Were they a couple at that time? I want to say yes, because they became a couple when I was right around that age. So, where was he? Or was it before KD entered our lives that Alvie chose to use me for oral sex? I'll never know that. Never. I know that the day Alvie Wilson forced himself on me is the first day of my life as I know it. It's a day in my life that I pray God will allow me to someday forget. I believe Alvie was nineteen when he did what he did. He must have thought that it wouldn't haunt me for the rest of my life.

Sarah never worried too much about who she left us with, as long as she could pass us off and go about her day (working hopefully) without being responsible for her children. One of those people was Yolanda, another great friend of hers. Yolanda was a very skinny woman, almost like a skeleton. I'm not exactly sure of her height, but even as a child, she didn't seem very big at all. She probably wasn't much more than five feet tall, with long hair that was so thin you could almost see her scalp. She also had a mouth full of false teeth that were too big for her small, boney face. She wouldn't always bother wearing them, but either way, she was very scary looking.

Yolanda had a young son named Jesse. I'm sure Jesse was slightly younger than us, but even as a child myself, I understood that he had some major behavioral problems. I don't doubt for one second that they developed from his toxic mother and her shit ways. I can remember being left with Yolanda at her apartment once and her pinning us between the wall and the couch so that we were unable to move. She had us positioned with our backs against the wall with the couch pushed against us so that we were fixed there and couldn't move. She could see us, and we could watch her, but we couldn't move. I am sure this was before my sister Sandra was born, as she is seven years younger than me. I don't remember her being there anyway, so I assume I was no older than seven. Either way, Yolanda had no time for extra kids while dealing with her own son. Maybe that's why she thought her actions were appropriate.

I remember Yolanda's dad too. We called him Pappy. He was a decrepit, bedridden old man who used to put his tongue in my mouth when we all had to line up to kiss him goodbye.

Chapter 3

After KD was in the picture, we moved around a little before we settled down into the house on 10th Street. We lived in Oklahoma City—a couple of times actually. Ralph and I went to school there at Willard Elementary. I remember Sarah putting me in brown shoes that were a couple of sizes too big, with the toes of them stuffed with socks as an attempt to keep them from falling off. For a time, we also lived in a homeless shelter in Oklahoma City that was referred to as the Jesus House. I don't know how long we were there, but we lived in a building full of people, all of them strangers, and with no privacy of any sort. It was basically a building full of huge rooms that were lined with cots for people to sleep on out in the open.

I remember having to leave our floor for another to get to the community bathroom; there was one for the men and one for the women. Everyone ate dinner downstairs in a cafeteria-type set up. I remember having to eat this meat-like product. I hoped it was meat. It was one of the most horrible things I've ever eaten. I'll never forget that smell.

We did manage to make friends with a couple of kids from the Jesus House: Stephany and Eric, who were twins. The only person Ralph and I both remember was a large black man named Ambros. He was always so nice to us. I remember that he would kind of watch out for us while KD was away. I believe Ambros was a truck driver. I remember he let Ralph and me in his cab once and him looking down at us from his seat. I don't know how long we had to stay in that shelter, but I know we never saw that nice man after that.

Our house at 537 North 10th Street in Ponca is where we lived the longest. We used to go across the street into the pet shop and get whatever candy was available in the machines. We could get handful of dusty candy for 25 cents. Ralph and I used to ride our bikes in the parking lot of that pet store and pretend that we were in a motorcycle gang. We weren't allowed inside much. If the sun was shining, and we weren't at school, then we were made to stay outside. Hanging out in the house just wasn't an option; it was that whole "children are to be seen and not heard" thing. Let's face it: We couldn't be silent, since we were kids, and if we weren't, we knew what was to come. As such, we actively preferred not to be around home and stayed away as much as possible, especially when our stepdad was there.

There were a million times, living in that house, when all I wanted and needed was a place I could escape to—like when we were being hit, or insulted and verbally degraded, or when we were being forced to massage Sarah and KD's naked bodies. That was so embarrassing for me, having a grown man, one who is supposed to be my protector, force me to put my hands on his naked skin. What in an adult man's mind would make him think that it was perfectly acceptable to get a body massage from a small child? Sarah and KD both thought that. Our own mother and the guy who'd vowed to protect us. It was normal for each of them to leave the bathroom in nothing but a towel, yell for a bottle of lotion to be found, lay down on a blanket still wrapped in nothing but a towel, and then proceed to make Ralph and me give their naked bodies a "rub down." We had to start at the shoulders and make our way all the way down to the feet. This was also to include the inner thigh area all the way up to the groin. I felt so disgusted every time KD's towel would "slip," and I'd be subjected to seeing his naked private area. No big deal for him. I mean, why not have small children do for you what normal adults pay other adults to do?

Our young eyes were not meant for seeing that, and our young hands were not meant to be used that way. I hated KD and still do. My little-girl hands were not meant for his satisfaction. And young-boy hands are not meant to rub lotion on the body of an adult woman, even if that woman is his mother. Sarah deserves the shit beaten right out of her.

Our life went on like that until one day, when I was roughly nine or ten years old, they came to us and said that they are going to get a divorce. This was in 1989/1990. KD had come to me and was trying to explain some shit about him and Sarah having adult problems (blah blah blah) and just because he was leaving didn't mean that he was leaving us and he loved us (blah blah blah). I can't begin to tell you what he was trying to say to me word for word, but I do remember how I felt: EXCITED!! I was so happy, listening to his pathetic voice tell me (insincerely) how he'd still be around, but he and Sarah just couldn't make it work. I thought I might actually laugh out loud at that, though I knew I better not (damnit). The overwhelming feeling of relief I felt, knowing that the abuse from him might be over, felt amazing.

After KD left, we stayed in that house on 10th Street for a while. I was too young to know what kind of situation they had worked out that allowed us to stay there. I knew that Sarah didn't own the house and neither did KD, so I figured someone must have been paying the bills for them to allow it. I learned much later that KD's dad was the property owner.

Sarah worked just down the highway as a clerk at a convenience store. She also waited tables at one point. That had really been her thing most of our lives, either working a register or waiting tables for tip money. She apparently had better customer-service skills than her parenting ones. As the oldest of the four kids, I guess I did okay in my role. I mean I had a lot of responsibility for the two younger kids, DJ and Sandra, and I think I did well for being so little. Along with that role of eldest sibling came other things.

Sarah was terrible about who she let us be around, with or without KD. I've had experience myself as a single mother of three now, which I will get into eventually. I understand how hard she had to work to make ends meet. I understand the trials and struggles. Being a single parent is difficult for anyone. It is no joke. But why not leave us with trusted people? Why not work hard at finding us someone to keep us safe until she got home? Perhaps that was too difficult for her. I don't know exactly who Sarah met first, but there were a lot of people we would have been better off without. Like the time when JohnBoy Apell pressed his erection against me. For some reason unknown to me, JohnBoy was left to babysit us. I doubt that I was eleven at the time. I was asleep on the bedroom floor when I was woken up by him. He was lying next to me on the floor with his body pressed firmly against mine. He was using me. He had his erection pushed firmly into my back while he breathed heavily down my neck. I was so fucking afraid of what was about to happen to me that I jumped up and ran into the bathroom. It was nighttime. I stayed in that bathroom until another adult came back. JohnBoy was a friend of Yolanda, Sarah's skinny friend, so maybe Sarah thought he was good enough to take care of me.

Then there was Dan, a guy that Sarah had dated around the same time that she and KD were divorcing. Right after we left 10th Street, before we left for Blackwell, we moved (with him and his teenaged son) into an apartment building still in Ponca City. The building had four apartments, two on the first floor and two on the second, none of them very large. These were very low-income, and nothing fancy by any means. The entire building was the size of a large house. There was, however, a door that led to a basement-type boiler room, set up for the entire building. That is where Ralph and I (not yet teenagers) would hang out with Dan's son. I'm sure he hated being there as much as we did. He didn't stay with us long though. He probably went back to his own mom. Dan stayed with us when his kid left.

I'll tell you one hundred times over that I have no idea how or where Sarah met these fucking weirdos, and with Dan being a heavy alcoholic, he was just as weird as the rest. I don't remember Dan ever having a real job while he was in our lives. His role seemed to be to stay with us while Sarah worked her retail job. I can't remember how long Dan was with us, but I do know that it was over a summer break from school. While Sarah worked, he would take us to the lake, and we would spend entire days there. It became routine that we would stop at Sarah's place of employment and grab snacks supplies while Dan got beer—cases of it.

Sarah worked and Dan watched us (with cases of beer). As the oldest of Sarah's four children, at eleven or twelve, I had to be the adult. At least, that's what Dan thought. So, this guy took it upon himself to make me his drinking buddy. I'm not kidding an ounce. After we'd spent the entire day at the lake, with Dan spending the day drinking, he'd pile all four of us and himself into his white single-cab truck, and we'd then stop back by Sarah's job for more food and alcohol before he would take us back home, where I was an "adult" and my siblings still children.

Then he and I would drink beer, with him encouraging me to drink mine as fast as possible. Then another for Dan and another for me. Obviously, my small body could not consume as much alcohol as his adult one, but that didn't stop him from encouraging me to keep up. He was trying to teach me to match him beer for beer. Dan was a shorter, stockier man. I'm going to say about five feet nine and a hundred and ninety pounds or so, with a definite beer belly. He had tanned skin (from being a fucking bum and laying around in the sun all day), hairy shoulders and chest, thick Coke-bottle glasses, and false teeth—I know this because I saw them come out once when he was yelling at Sarah. Dan always, always, always had on blue-jean cut-off shorts that (even in the early nineties) were too short for a man. People and their weird-ass shit.

Anyway, after I was good and hammered, Dan would sit me on his lap and tell me that we were going to "talk about the first thing that pops up." That guy kept me drunk that whole summer it seemed. For being such a small-framed child, I got good at not throwing up. I was even able to drink vodka and orange juice like a champ.

It was also in this same timeframe that the JohnBoy Apell situation happened. I did tell Sarah and Dan what happened. I remember Dan yelling and causing a ruckus in the next room like he was concerned. Neither of them was that concerned though. No police came to take a report, Sarah never talked to me about it after the fact, and I was offered no therapy or even a hug. It was just another day that we moved on from like nothing ever happened.

I don't know why Dan and Sarah split up. I bet it didn't have anything to do with the fact that he tried to keep me drunk so that he could sit me down on his lap and keep me talking so I wouldn't pay attention to the fact that he was rubbing me around on his erection. It was probably more the fact that he was a jobless loser, and she was a whore. Not compatible, I suppose.

Then there was James Wallace, whom I assume Sarah met through her place of employment, just as she met most other people. James Wallace was a nice-looking guy who dressed just as nice. He never appeared sloppy or out of sorts when he came around. He had a nice smile, showing off lots of teeth. While Sarah worked, James started to hang around some to check on us and make sure we were okay. He was in his early twenties (at least), old enough to have a job and his own place to live. He was a fun guy too. He laughed a lot, which made us laugh too. We didn't mind him being around. Even when Sarah was home, James would stick around. Did she make friends with James? Did she invite him to hang out or did he invite himself and she just didn't make him leave? He mainly just hung around and watched cartoons with us. Like I said, James was in his early twenties, and I was twelve or thirteen. That's about the time it got down.

Sarah had zero concern for James being around us. Did she think that James was her friend and that he was doing her a favor? Did she think that maybe something was in the works between them? I don't know what Sarah thought. She needed to have her damn head examined, because she made shitty choices for us once again with James and was responsible for every action that took place.

I lost my virginity to James Wallace when I was twelve or thirteen years old. Like totally gone. He took it all. I lost my virginity before my period even came.

One day, James took me to his house and lay me down on what I believe to be the living-room floor. I remember that another adult male walked right past me, and as he did so, he looked down right into my face. He knew what was about to happen to me. I didn't see him again after that moment. James lay me down, took off my bottoms, and began to perform oral sex on me. By this time in my short life, I had been around enough dirty people to know what was happening.

In any case, I braced myself for what was about to happen with James. I don't know why I didn't try to fight him off. I don't know why I didn't try to save myself. I was so embarrassed that

I wanted to cry. At one point, I didn't know what my body was doing and thought that I peed on him. I kept my tears to myself. When he finished there, he climbed on top of my small frame and penetrated me vaginally and took my virginity from me.

When it was all over, it didn't seem like a big deal. He just took me back to Sarah's house where I acted like nothing at all had happened. Something had happened though. James Wallace, who was at least nine years older than me, raped my small body. He made me feel like he wanted to be my "boyfriend," and then he had adult sex with me. He completely took away whatever was left of me that could be called a child. As if Alvie hadn't caused enough damage.

James used to come over to hang out with me specifically, even before he took my virginity. Once, when the lights were off, James and I were lying on the floor under a blanket, watching a Disney movie—I won't ruin your day by telling you which one. James had his erection pressed against me and was feeling my body with his hands. I don't know where my siblings were. I don't know where Sarah was. I just know where I was.

I didn't make him stop. I should have. A healthy child mind would know that those actions were wrong in the worst way. Not mine though. I accepted it as normal behavior. I didn't know just how much he wasn't supposed to be doing that to me. I was an easy target for James. I'd just spent the last seven years of my life living with KD, a person I was sure was the devil, and I displayed all the typical signs of being abused in a broken, single-mom household. The perfect target for a child-sex predator.

The day I told Sarah what had happen with James and me, it was very matter of fact. She and I were sitting in her front seat of her car about to get out when I said it out loud: "James had sex with me." I was so scared that she would be angry with me, but as it turned out, I had no reason to be scared. She wasn't upset at all. She didn't so much as blink or say a word. I had just confessed to her that James had raped me, and her response to that was to turn towards the door, look back at me for only a second, and then exit the car. She never said one word to me about it then or anytime afterwards. Though I do specifically remember her saying, at some point later, "James couldn't get with me, so he got with my daughter instead." I wish I remember who it was that she said that to, right in front of me. I wish I knew who the other man was who looked down at me right before I was raped. Why did he let that happen? Was I in a house with two pedophiles? Why did Sarah not care enough about me to take the proper actions and call the authorities? Sadly, it's because she just didn't care.

Next, I'll tell you about Mel, who was the boyfriend of Brenda, another one of Sarah's friends. I remember meeting Brenda and her daughter Penny in 1990 or 1991. I met Penny first. She was nineteen and crazy wild. She also had a toddler son, whom I heard eventually moved to California where he was killed. Anyway, now that I'm an adult, I understand that Mel wasn't really anyone's boyfriend. Mel hung around a lot, and I knew that he was sleeping with Sarah.

The first time I ever smoked pot was in that house on 10th Street with Mel. Sarah was with us, and so was my little brother Ralph. All this took place around the same time, so I was twelve or thirteen years old. Whatever. I was all for it. Mel seemed like a cool guy. I liked him. He made us all laugh. It was cool that Sarah had found this guy who wasn't mean to us. When he visited the house on 10th Street, which wasn't too frequently, he'd bring us toys and cook food for us! Heck yeah! This is cool right? Mel was way different than KD, because Mel thought we were good kids. I can't be sure of exactly when it was that Mel raped me for the first time, but I'm positive it was after we left the house on 10th Street and moved to Blackwell, Oklahoma.

Our house there was two stories with a long, narrow, carpeted stairway that led to the two bedrooms on the second floor. All the rooms in the house, including the kitchen and bathroom, were small and carpeted, apart from the dining-room/living-room area, which made up one massive open room. Sarah worked the night shift at a convenience store in Blackwell, and by this time, Ralph and I were primarily responsible for our younger siblings.

One night while Sarah was at work, someone came in through our backdoor and stole my little sister from the couch we were all sleeping on. I was awakened afterwards by her crying and telling me that she had woken up to find a man carrying her down the alleyway outside. Luckily, when she woke up and screamed, the man let go of her, and she was able to make her way back home. I'll never know what else might have happened with my sister as I lay there sleeping on that couch, but after my sister woke me up, I gathered all my siblings and walked them across town, in the dark, to the convenience store where Sarah was working. After that incident, Sarah started having Mel stay with us. I'm not sure, but I still ask myself an eerie question: Could Mel have set this up? We would have never known if he did. Exactly who was it that had intruded in our home?

Chapter 4

Mel was a California guy. Very hyper. He was always just kind of hopping around. Anxiety ridden, if I had to guess. He was short in stature with a thin frame, and he had brown hair that he kept feathered back on the side and very neat, with what's called a rat's tail in the back. Mel tried to have this sort of Mexican gangster persona. He was also a good-looking guy with a charm that the hood-rat women loved, and he smelled of Old English Leather musk. He had no trouble getting women, but Mel liked Sarah, so he started hanging around. We were in a house in Blackwell by this time, which was literally the next town over from Ponca and sadly the town where I was born. That is where my sister was taken from the couch and when Mel started to hang around a lot more.

One day, I heard a banging on the front door and heard a fuming woman screaming Mel's name outside. I opened the door, and she took off up the stairs to the bedroom where Sarah and Mel lay asleep. I bet Sarah was shocked beyond words when she woke up to Brenda, Mel's alleged girlfriend, slapping the shit out of her. At thirteen years old, and still having loyalty to Sarah, I grabbed Brenda with all my might and tried to stop her from hitting Sarah's face. Everything ended then, and Mel left with Brenda. Of course, Mel having Brenda didn't stop him from inserting himself into our single-parent family. He was around so damn much that I fully believed that he was not with Brenda anymore and was in a full-time relationship with Sarah.

Like I said before, Mel was a likeable guy. He brought us toys, cooked us food, and even spent quality time with us. Mel had a good dog too, a great big golden-tan ridgeback dog named Varmett. He was very well trained. Mel could tell that dog to do anything, and he would do it. It was an open rumor amongst Sarah's wicked group of people that one of those bitches let both Mel and his dog fuck her. I heard the adults talking about it. Nobody ever tried to protect us from hearing their more-than-disgusting conversations.

Anyway, we were super impressed by this dog. He was friendly to all of us. So, now we had Mel, who was a super-cool stepdad guy, and we had a family pet. Wow! Then one day, Varmett wasn't so good and did his business inside the house. It was crazy, because he was such a smart and well-trained dog that he could've easily let someone know he needed to go out. I want to say that he got left in the house while we were out, and we came home to a mess, but I can't really remember.

Poor Varmett. Mel became so enraged at him that he took out the pocketknife that he always wore on his side and stabbed Varmett multiple times. We all just watched with sadness. After Mel handed down punishment to the dog, he then carried Varmett upstairs and lay him down on one of the bedroom floors. Varmett was lucky none of the stab wounds had killed him. Mel made me sit right there and hold that dog's head while he sewed him up with a needle and thread. I just sat there and did as I was told.

Honestly, I don't know why Varmett was so brutally punished in the first place. He didn't do anything worse to our carpets than what was already there. Remember how I described the Wilson house? Sarah and Elaine Wilson were best friends and the same kind of people with the same disgusting habits. Our house was filthy every . . . single . . . day. I swear on my life that I can't remember Sarah ever doing so much as running a vacuum. Our floors stayed covered in dog feces all the time (though none of it came from Varmett except that once). I honestly can't remember what kind of dogs we even had, but I remember dog shit being left on the floor for so long that, by the time she finally made one of us clean it up, it had already dried and stuck to the carpet. She sure wasn't going to do it. She wasn't doing anything as a matter of fact. Ever. Not in the house anyway.

She could, I must admit, keep a job. There wasn't a time when Sarah didn't have a job, because there wasn't ever a time that our house was cleaned. Sarah worked, and so by that logic alone, it was *our* job to keep up with the housework. She said it so many times that I wanted to punch her in the face. I got so sick of hearing it. "What do you think I had kids for?" *Um . . . because you're a whore!*

Our house was infested with roaches. As a matter of fact, every house we ever had to share with Sarah had roaches. They were under and behind everything: inside picture frames; in the corners of every wall; under all the paneling and wallpaper; in the light fixtures and sockets; in the kitchen cabinets; and under, in, and behind the stove and the refrigerator both. We had roaches in every single part of our home. Probably because Sarah was (and still is) a lazy human being.

She had absolutely no problems living in filth and zero concerns about us—the children she was supposed to love and protect—living in that exact same filth. She had four children by this point and that meant she was responsible for their wellbeing, including providing them with clean shelter. Not for Sarah, no, no, no. And not for us either. Sarah did not take care of our laundry needs. Ralph and I used to wash out our laundry in the bathtub with dishwashing liquid. We worked as a team. We'd wash and wring everything out by hand and then hang it all around the house to dry, because we had no washing machine or dryer or a mother who was willing to provide us with clean laundry.

Ralph and I were very small children, so it was often difficult for us to wring clothes out well enough to keep them from dripping water onto the carpet. Even with Ralph on one end of the pair of jeans or towel and me at the other end, twisting in opposite directions, we didn't do that great of job. We did try though. Still, after our clothing finally did dry, our clothes were stiff and smelled of dish soap and our disgusting house. Damn it, that sucked so bad. Guess how many times that I had to wear damp clothes to school, which made the odor even worse. Guess how noticeable my smell was to the other girls who were young too but mean enough to push me around for it.

Sarah didn't clean the kitchen ever. We always had piles of dirty dishes with dried or moldy food filling the sink, and a constant swarm of flies everywhere. *"What do you think I had you kids for?"* The garbage didn't go out. The can was piled with trash until it overflowed onto the floor, and instead of it being picked up, it just was kicked around instead. It wasn't uncommon to find maggots in our kitchen either. Again, another odor created. The stove was never without shit stuck to it, with grease, dirt, and spills from pots and pans never being cleaned but rather forming one layer of mess on top of another inside and around the burner rings. And forget about looking into the refrigerator.

The bathroom and every other common area of our home was equally filthy. Yes, Ralph and I could have done more as far as housework was concerned, but we were doing what we could to even survive by this point. Head lice was forever a huge issue for all of us, for just about my entire childhood, though mainly for my sister and I, because we had the long hair. Ralph and I had darker skin and hair than our sisters, thanks to our Native American heritage, so the lice were easier to see on us. I endured a lot of grief at school because I had head lice and couldn't help it. I would spend hours combing it out. Bugs and eggs filled my hair. I'd do everything I could to try and make it go away. Ralph and I did the same for the younger two siblings.

It was difficult to control the lice situation as kids when Sarah didn't care an ounce. She would buy us the lice shampoo, but then she'd stop right there. She would not take any further steps to rid us of our problem. I know I keep saying that Sarah wouldn't do shit, but I can't express to you how much she neglected us. We needed Sarah, and she had shit to do for us. There was no treatment of our rooms, no washing of our bedding, no washing of our laundry, nothing! WE ALWAYS HAD LICE! I was poor, brown, and dirty, I was filled with lice, and my clothes smelled like shit because my mother was a lazy bitch who was not motivated to lift a finger to provide her children with a cleaner environment, and that made going to school tough. Sarah made me a target in more ways than one, but I'll get to that soon enough.

She was (and is) a dirty woman with a filthy house, dirty kids, and absolutely nothing to offer anyone, financially or domestically, so why did Mel want to be with her? He was a decent-looking guy. He surely could have gotten a better woman than Sarah. He could have gotten a different woman at least, and later he did, but still . . . why Sarah?

She herself was also dirty, her teeth were bad, and I know that (if we had lice as bad as we did) she must have had lice as well. No doubt. And she wouldn't or couldn't cook a real meal, which of course was why we liked Mel coming around, as he did cook for us. That sort of made it worth him being there. Sarah had food stamps but still never seemed to have any food in the house. Having minimal to no food made it hard to be happy. The state of Oklahoma was helping her to provide for us, but we didn't have anything in the house that wasn't hot dogs, bologna, white bread, and the ever-so-popular ramen noodles. Did it suck that Sarah didn't know how to cook? Yes, it absolutely did, but at the very least, she could have brought real food into the house. I guess that, since she didn't plan on preparing meals for us, she must not have seen the need.

Ralph and I got sufficient at providing for ourselves. Damn, all we wanted was real food. The kind of food we had seen at other people's houses. I know for a fact that this wasn't too much to ask for. I am a mother and a grandmother now, and I know that (in both roles) I am supposed to provide everything possible, including basic nutrition. We didn't have to be hungry. Sarah had means to provide food for us. Even if she had no cash money, she still had a way to provide food, but because she's so selfish and lazy, it just wasn't something she could do for her own children.

I was hungry many times, especially after Sarah and KD split. In the cabinets, we did have yellow boxes of Always Save macaroni, which I would have been grateful for if she would put an ounce of care into cooking it. Sarah could not cook, and she didn't care to learn. As well, we had boxes of off-brand helpers, something she could add tuna or ground meat to and call it a day. She was a terrible cook. When she was married to KD and still *had to* cook, everything she prepared was the worst because she put forth no effort. Now, she only had children, whose opinions she cared nothing about, so her laziness got worse and so had her concern about food. She just didn't care if we got any.

I honestly believe in my soul that providing for us was just a huge inconvenience to her. She would occasionally attempt to throw together some slop, complain of how badly her feet hurt from working all day, then retreat to the wallowed-out hole in her chair and demand we get to the dishes. Sometimes it was worth being hungry just so that I didn't have to choke down whatever her option might be. Sarah's food stamps were worthless to us if she wasn't going to use them correctly. We wanted and needed protein. We needed real meat, which is why Ralph and I took it upon ourselves to get some, becoming very good at filling our oversized coats with food that we didn't pay for.

This was in the very early nineties in a small town, so it was easier for us than I'm sure it would be today. I was in charge of getting the meat. I could easily pull a package of pork chops into my jacket and be out of the door with no problems. Why always pork chops? I don't know. Maybe it was an easier set up for the taking, and anyway, we just liked pork chops. Ralph took care of our cigarette addiction, which we absolutely had. Between the two of us, we were also able to keep some candy stashed away. Normally it was a giant bar of solid chocolate—again, just because it was easier for the taking.

Should we have been in those stores stealing food and cigarettes? No, of course not. Did we have to survive a different lifestyle? Yes, we did. Our trips to the market without Sarah became a normal thing. Did she ever really pressure us about where the food we were preparing for ourselves had come from? Nope. I'm sure she got some kind of relief knowing we did it ourselves. We deserved those cigarettes, and we enjoyed smoking them. That was our avenue of relief.

When Mel was there, it was different, because he brought food to cook! We thought he was the best cook ever. He prepared steaks and potatoes, along with vegetables that were not from a can. Sarah firmly believes that there are only two vegetables: canned corn and canned green beans. We got steaks with steak sauce instead of our dried porkchops with ketchup. When Mel was there, we got real food. Not too much to ask, but still . . . it was something that we normally lacked.

A lot of the time, Mel brought laughter into our house too. He tried to connect with us. Although Mel himself was very clean and put together, he never seemed to care that our house was a total garbage can. Often it was Mel who provided our candies and desserts, but our gifts from Mel did not come without a price, which I will get to shortly. He was always willing to go retrieve our desserts from the local store and bring us the things we wanted. Of course, he didn't mind because he cared for us. Right? With me being the oldest child, I was normally recruited to go along with Mel to help bring back our treats.

He had a long, white, four-door car, some kind of Lincoln I think. It had a full backseat as well as a full front seat, that was one long seat from the driver to the passenger door. Mel liked it that I sat very close to him while he drove. That made it easier for him to touch my body. He'd drive with his left hand and assault me with his right. We never just went to the store and right back home again. Each time, he felt the need to park us someplace private. It allowed for him to kiss me. It allowed private time for him to be able to undo my pants and work his way into my panties as far as he needed to be able to penetrate my thirteen-year-old body with his hands. He trained me to masturbate him while he did the same to me. He also would talk me through it every time. Mel liked to give me instructions on what to do and how to please him.

He always told me how beautiful I was, and how he loved me and always would. He'd tell me I was perfect, that any guy in the world would be lucky to have me, and tell me how sad he would be when I grew older and left his company for someone younger than him. I always thought to myself, *Why would I do that? Mel loves us all. Right? I mean, look what he does for us all the time.* I thought Mel was perfect for us. I just had to give him something in return.

When we'd finally return from the "store," whether Sarah was there or not, nobody ever asked us what took so long. Sarah never asked why we were gone for twenty minutes when the store was a two-minute drive away. Mel said that I shouldn't say anything to Sarah, because of course, she might be upset with me, and "We don't want her upset, right?"

Though there were a couple of times with Mel when I was very scared and embarrassed, sex with him quickly became normal. By the time I was thirteen or fourteen years old, I was pro at adult sex. Mel showed me everything I needed to know. I knew how to relax myself so that I was able to endure his entire self. It always made him smile to talk about how well I did. He talked me through how to give a proper blowjob. He said men wouldn't love me if I couldn't "make them feel love." He also taught me how to take oral sex after I climaxed, so that he didn't have to stop and could continue to make me "feel like a woman."

Sometimes I did feel ashamed though, like one time out driving in Mel's car with Ralph and his buddy Andrew in the backseat. I was in the front with Mel, and he unzipped his pants, made me lean over, and proceeded to have me give him oral sex—all with my brother and his friend behind us in the backseat. I was so scared . . . sick to my stomach with worry that the guys could see me and knew what I was doing.

For so much of that ride, Mel had me down on his penis. When I sat up, I did not dare turn around. I just knew in my heart that they knew exactly what had happened and had seen me. I count this day as one of the most embarrassing of my life. I cried. I was somehow able to get past it quickly though. Mel was always there to assure me I was beautiful and had done a good job for him. That I was perfect. Me? Young, dirty, smelly, and full of lice? Perfect for Mel?

Another time—I remember it being late at night—Mel was at our house, but I don't think Sarah was home. It was dark in the house except for the light from the TV in the living area. That particular night, there happened to be other people sleeping over. I still find it beyond my comprehension that other people were willing to sleep inside my house. I guess even low-life kids like us sometimes managed to have low-life buddies.

There were probably three or four people lying around under blankets on the floor in the living area, watching TV in the dark room. Mel had me off of the floor, bent over the back of the recliner, fucking me from behind while a room full of people lay in front of us. I was scared to death that someone would get up to turn on the light and find me in such an awful position. Nobody did get up though. Mel was inside me and using me to climax, while I had to take it all without making a sound. He'd had me in that position many times, doing to me whatever he pleased while I was forbidden to make a sound. He eventually finished doing what he needed to do to me, and that was that.

Even though Mel was careful not to be caught with me (I think), there was a time that I know for a fact someone saw us. Mel had me sitting on his lap. I had on a nightgown, and Mel had his fingers inside of my vagina. He was doing to me what was only normal for us: molesting and being molested. I don't know how long this person had been watching, but when I climbed off Mel's lap, stood up, and turned around, someone was watching through the triangle piece of glass in the front door. I don't know how long they had been standing there, but when they saw me, they immediately ran away. To this day, I don't know who it was that was watching me get molested. Nobody ever came forward and talked to me about it. It's something that I'll never forget. I don't know how to gain closure over something like that. It tortures me, just like not knowing who it was that looked down at me that day with James Wallace.

I am sure you can guess that I am not the only child that Mel was molesting. Like I said, even though I was poor, dirty trash, there were people willing to come around. Like Chrystal and Beverly. Chrystal's brother (I think) hung out with mine, so she just hung around too. And Beverly was another girl like me who had no friends. I never knew anything about her home life. I just knew that she was willing to hang out at my house.

Chrystal was blonde and tall for her age, and Beverly was shorter and a bit heavy set. She had solid black hair, styled in a bowl cut that didn't come to her shoulders, and very pale skin. I remember that she also had round cheeks and a funny laugh that made me laugh. Maybe she hung out at my house because she wasn't forced to deal with judgement there. Sadly, instead of judgement, she got something worse, as did the tall blonde.

One of those nights when Sarah was gone and Mel was there to keep us, I caught him masturbating the tall blonde. Again, it was dark, the TV was on, and we were all laying on the floor under a blanket. Two thirteen- or fourteen-year-old girls under a blanket with Mel, a thirty-something-year-old man, in between them. Of course, he had his corduroy pants completely open with his penis all the way out for me to be touching. At one point, I sat up and saw his other hand moving around on her body under that blanket, and she was obviously experiencing something. I got so upset with the both of them. Why? Because he had me convinced that he was in love with me. Why did he need another girl?

Mel dealt with the situation just like he would with any other. He lied. He lied and told me that I hadn't seen what I obviously *had* seen. He was eventually able to calm things down, get us back under the blanket on the floor, and continued to sexually assault the both of us at the same time. Once he had his hands down my pants and into my vagina, I no longer paid attention to the fact that she was getting the same treatment on the other side of him. She and I were molested at the same time that night. After that, she developed a crush on Mel, so she was over at our house as much as possible, and Mel took full advantage every time she came around. Apparently, she didn't know any better either. I don't know what ever happened to her.

Poor Beverly hadn't wanted that though. I know that she had to have been so scared. Our house had two stories, and at the top back of the second story was a balcony. That is where it went down for her. I don't know many details except that he had Beverly up there and was doing what child molesters do, trying to have his way with her young body. Unlike Chrystal or myself, she told someone what had happened to her at my house, and the authorities came. I honestly don't know what came of it though, if anything at all. I do know that it ended any kind of friendship I had with Beverly.

At school, things were changing for Beverly by way of social status, and rumor had gotten around about what had happened to her at my house, so whatever kind of shitty treatment I was receiving before just intensified. I can't tell you how many fist-fights I got into. People hated me. They wanted to beat me up because my clothes smelled horrible and didn't fit me. They wanted to beat me up, along with relentless bullying, because I was constantly infested with lice. They wanted to beat me up because I was awkward as fuck (circumstances you know), and I didn't seem to fit in with anyone. They wanted to beat me up because I wasn't nice—I didn't like other people any more than they liked me.

Beverly, with her status changing, felt empowered, and that led to her being as mean to me as possible. She hated me for what had happened to her at my house. She didn't ask for it. She didn't deserve to be abused. And she needed to take out her anger and pain on someone, and that someone was me. Why wouldn't it be me? Girls are cruel.

One day in particular turned out to be the roughest. I had been in a lot of fights leading up to that day. I had no choice. I was an easy target and none of the staff gave a fuck about me. I'm sure I had to be wearing some kind of stress on my face that any kind of human could have noticed. I just don't know why no one did. Was I not showing signs of abuse yet? I was already thirteen or fourteen years into it. Surely the signs had to be there.

My fight with Beverly was pretty brutal. I was in the nineth grade at that point. I had been dealing with bullying and this sort of shit my entire life. I'd been molested, beaten, and had psychological games played with my mind for as far back as I could remember, and a girl can only take so much before she snaps. I snapped for the first time on poor Beverly. At that moment, I was so extremely aggressive that I could do nothing to make myself stop. I am so sorry for that to this day. Like I said, Beverly had plenty of reasons to hate me stemming from just one night at my house. She had been coaxed into being abusive to me and was just as much a victim as I was.

The buildup to my snapping started early in the day. She sat behind me in class and pulled my hair. Then I could feel things being spat into my hair. I screamed at her to stop, and the people around just snickered. Nobody gave a shit, and they thought that it was funny. Even the teacher only addressed me for my outburst, ignoring what had caused it. In the mindset of children, it is commonly accepted behavior to pick on the kid who is about to lose her mind. Nobody knows why she's starting to lose it or cares to ask. That day, nobody knew that inside of me was a child that had been dying for years, before she had the chance to even *be* a child, before she ever had the chance to know anything about a "normal" childhood—the chance to be a normal, happy little girl. My whole life, I'd slowly been made to understand that happiness and normalcy wasn't something that was meant for me. I was meant for a different purpose.

That day, I begged Beverly to stop, feeling the rage building up in my body. But after class ended, Beverly approached me in the hallway and gave me a shove. That was all that it took to wake up the monster that had been seeded in me so many years before by

Alvie, my first sexual abuser. Hatred like no child should ever feel erupted within me. At that moment, I went truly insane.

After it was over, there was blood that wasn't mine. I'd taken everything out on Beverly, giving her every bit of pain that had been given to me for so many years—another thing she didn't deserve. After the situation was over, it was clear that I was at fault. Of course, I was. I didn't see her again after that day. Only a short while later, I was gone from Blackwell. The police came to my house that afternoon. They asked me what had happened at school that day, and I told them. I didn't get to tell them *why* I was such an angry beast of a kid. Nobody asked why (or even how) I was able to do so much damage to another person as I was just a tiny human myself.

I didn't volunteer any explanation because secrets . . . you know. We're not allowed to tell anyone our secrets. Sarah talked to the police for just a couple of minutes, and then they left. Damn Sarah was so pissed at me. I didn't care though. Not much mattered to me anymore.

Chapter 5

Mel had this friend named Johnnie, who was just the same kind of cat as Mel, with the same kind of attitude and persona, and though he was younger than Mel, he was yet another grown man who was willing to rape a child.

Johnnie was in his early twenties when we met, but he looked much older. He was a big guy. Taller and heavier than Mel, with square shoulders, reddish hair, and a scar below his rib cage that was so long it wrapped nearly halfway around his body. He said he got it from a fight. I don't know if that was the truth, but it sure was impressive to a thirteen- or fourteen-year-old girl like me. He did look a bit rough for being in his twenties, but I assume now that it was his shitty lifestyle that stole his youthful looks. At the time though, I didn't give it any thought. I was already so used to hanging out with adults that his looks and age didn't raise any red flags for me.

Mel was around all the time, and then Johnnie was too, and stayed after Mel just sort of drifted away and stopped coming around. It was strange. Mel was like a fixture in our home for a couple of years, and then it seemed, like one day, he was just gone. I can't remember the last time I saw Mel's face in person.

Unfortunately, he didn't make his exit from our lives before molesting my little sister, Sandra, and to this day, she blames me for not saving her from Mel. She doesn't blame her mother. She blames me. The truth is that I could have saved her if I hadn't already been taught to be so silent.

Johnnie was around so much that, by the time I was well into my fourteenth year, it was openly known that Johnnie and I were having sex, and he was considered my boyfriend. I was fourteen and my boyfriend was in his twenties. Any of the mothers reading this upset yet? It also wasn't a secret that Johnnie already had a wife and son in the surrounding area. That didn't seem to be enough for Sarah to make him leave.

Johnnie told me daily how much he loved me and how his wife was an evil person. Johnnie even brought his sister Brandi to be part of our family. She was eighteen with a young child herself. It also turned out that she liked my brother in the same way that Johnnie liked me. He wasn't ready for that and never asked for it. A twelve- or thirteen-year-old male cannot consent to an adult woman. Do you know who consented for him? You wouldn't think it would be his own mother, but of course, it was. Sarah didn't give a shit what was going on as long as she didn't have to deal with us. She didn't have to either. We were always dealt with by other random people or pedophiles, whichever happened to be there.

Shortly after things went down at school with Beverly, I was moved out of Sarah's house and into an apartment with Loony Linda. Linda wasn't anyone that had any relation to us; she was just someone Sarah knew. We called her Loony Linda, because although she was able to live on her own, she definitely had some impairments—impairments that probably shouldn't have allowed for a fourteen-year-old crazy girl to live with her. But Sarah wasn't much for caring about someone else's wellbeing. Sarah took advantage of Linda. Having these impairments, she didn't have a job. She wasn't able to have one so that put her on a fixed income. She should not have had to be responsible for anything to do with me, but unfortunately, she did. That's how little Sarah cares for people. I was out of her hair for the time being, so she felt no need to bring any food or supplies for me. Sarah didn't pay Linda to allow me to stay or do anything else to provide for me while I was living with a lady who was not my mother and with whom I had no way to defend myself if I had to.

Johnnie eventually came to stay with Linda and me as well. Should he have? Again, hell no. I was happy to have Johnnie there with me though, because *Johnnie loves me, right?* He let me know how much he loved me each night that he lay beside me on the floor and did to me the things that others who'd loved me the same way had done.

By this time, I knew exactly what to do in return. Between Mel and Johnnie, I was well aware of my duty as a female. They taught me every part of a man's body and what to do with it. If I messed up, then just like a teacher with a student, they let me know what I'd done wrong and then walked me through the process of how to correct myself. Mel had been especially good at this. He liked talking to me. He liked to instruct me out loud. It was important for him that I be perfect. My role was that of "a woman." Anyway, only a little time went by before Johnnie and I ended up having to leave Linda's. We weren't supposed to be there in the first place, so we were made to leave. I went back to the house in Blackwell to ask Sarah if Johnnie and I both could come back into the house. Sarah agreed. "Yes," to me and "yes" to my twenty-something boyfriend.

I didn't see Mel again after 1994. Then one day, Johnnie left for a job and never returned. He did call me on the phone one day shortly after and said that he would be gone for a while and didn't know when he would be returning. I cried so much. I cried my eyes out, because I loved Johnnie so much. He was my best friend in my dysfunctional shit life. I missed him so much every day. My heart was broken when he left. I couldn't understand what I had done wrong. Even though he said that he needed to be gone for work, I still could not wrap my mind around why he'd leave me there. Both of his sisters entertained me with the notion of how much he loved me, and reassured me that, of course, he'd come back someday.

After Johnnie left, Paul Archer showed up, but the difference was that Paul was there only for Sarah. He was a tall, skinny, lazy-eyed, stringy-haired hillbilly son-of-a-bitch from Arkansas. One more time, I have to say, I still don't know how she does it. *How does she find them?* She attracts scum-of-the-earth people. He hated all four of us children, but before I knew it, Sarah was marrying him. This made him husband number four—Robert H., Leonardo, KD, and now Paul Archer. He couldn't stand any of us, and the feeling was mutual.

Paul would get so upset if Sarah had to give us any attention at all. Not that she gave us much, but he did his best to sever anything that was there between us and Sarah. Any relationship we had with her was purposefully disrupted by her new husband. He did what he could to drive a wedge between us. He despised the fact that we existed and did absolutely nothing to hide his dislike for us. He always talked about how we made things "harder for your mother." In return, we made it equally as hard for him to be there.

Why does a person marry someone with kids if they hate children? Instead of him being with a woman with zero kids, he married Sarah with four! He married her, and we got the bullshit end of the deal. AGAIN.

Paul, our new stepdad, was successful later at getting rid of the two younger siblings. He did everything he could to convince Sarah to send them to KD, their own father, and finally something worked. I can't say with an honest heart that Paul was 100 percent at fault for the kids having to leave. Sarah was/is a toxic mother, so it would have been easy for KD to prove her unfit in court. Also, surely, she wasn't supposed to take the kids out of Oklahoma, and she had done so. That was bad on her part. KD himself was in and out of our lives for a while around the time Paul started coming around. Not like in and out of our house, but we'd see him. He would come around, at least before Sarah married Paul and before KD himself got a different wife.

I couldn't believe it. KD had disappeared from our lives when they got divorced back in 1989/1990, and now he just randomly showed back up four fucking years later? Well, that was because they were sleeping together again. Of course they were. She was cheating on Paul with KD. I have to roll my fucking eyes. Go figure. They both are disgusting. That's not my problem though. That's on her. He didn't give a shit about me or Ralph either. Remember all that "just because me and your momma don't love each other doesn't mean I'm leaving you kids" bullshit? Oh, okay. Sure thing, KD. He only barely came around, and it was only for one thing.

That said, only twice did KD give me any bother after he and Sarah divorced and he was no longer my stepdad. Once he yelled at me for smoking pot. Sarah told him that I was being a bad kid and that he needed to have a talk with me. He did too. He chewed all over my ass about my pot smoking. He told me that he knew "I was fucking Johnnie" and there was nothing he could do to stop that, but if he heard I was pot smoking, he was going to come and give me an ass whooping.

So . . . that was what made sense to him, our concerned former stepdad. He should have been having that conversation with the guy who was raping me! He "couldn't" do anything to stop it? How about calling the police and reporting the fact that he was in his twenties and sexually engaged with a minor? No, they put that on me. KD and my own mother. They refused to see that

I had been fully taken advantage of in every sense of the word and chose to believe instead that I was being a slutty, drug-using teenaged inconvenience. Way to pay attention to your daughter, Sarah. Of course, I really was smoking pot. She wasn't wrong. I was smoking all the pot that was given to me.

The other time he bothered me was when he was over at our house, cheating on his woman with Sarah. Yes, they had divorced for whatever reason but were still trashy enough to sleep around with each other while in relationships with other people. I probably wouldn't know about it if they hadn't been so openly fucking grotesque about it. A match made in hell those two. I was in my room minding my own business when Sarah appeared in my doorway. I don't know what she was thinking. I never know what she's thinking though because her mind is so diluted with trash. Whatever it was, it was enough to make her say something to the effect of: "Would you like to join us in bed?"

As disgusting as I'm sure it was, I can't help but wonder how the request came about. What was that conversation like? My heart, mind, and gut want to believe that it was KD who initiated the thought. Why would Sarah? She's my mother. She birthed me. I am her first-born child and oldest daughter. Why would she think of that? She and I are supposed to share a bond like no other. But I'll truly never know if it was that bitch who came up with the idea to offer me up. I was fourteen years old when Sarah entered my bedroom with an unsure expression on her face, and then, in a shaky voice, asked me if I would like to join her and KD in her bedroom.

People mend relationships all the time, but it was on this day—at this moment—that our mother-daughter relationship was severed clean down the middle. I felt my heart shatter as I listen to my own mother's request. I couldn't believe what I was hearing. I already knew what was going on behind those doors, and it was nothing but foul. But still. My mother, the woman who had birthed me and the man who had been my evil stepdad for seven years wanted me to join them in a threesome. I just looked at her in that horrible moment and asked her sorry ass to leave my room.

She didn't have to do it. Didn't have to ask me that. Nobody forced those words to come from her. I think the right thing would have been for her to tell KD to get the fuck out and never return. That isn't what she did though. Instead, she did her part in breaking my heart that day. All the events leading up to that day, I had been able to put on the backburner, so to speak. I had found some place in the back of my mind to keep them. My own memory box. On that day though, in just that ten-second conversation between Sarah and me, they all resurfaced and shattered my fourteen-year-old soul—for the first time, anyway. It turns out that I am tougher than I thought, because I would have plenty more soul crushers in my future. I just didn't know it yet.

This next bit was a bit fuzzy for me, so my brother Ralph had to help me out some, answering my questions, because even though there are so many things about our past that stand out as clearly to me as if they just happened yesterday, there are also events and people that I hardly remember at all. It's odd the way our human brains works—the dates and times it chooses to remember and the ones it doesn't. That is what happens when an adult purposefully messes with a child's mind. When so much trauma is inflicted, the brain doesn't get the opportunity to develop in a healthy manner. It is disrupted.

Ralph says that we all traveled to Arkansas for Paul's family reunion—Paul's family who already weren't accepting of us brown-skinned, dirty little kids. I'm not exactly sure how many days we were there, but I know that every day we were forced to be there was bullshit. I remember the ugly faces they'd make at us. Maybe it was because Paul's own family didn't like him, so being his step-kids, we were just an additional dislike. I can't be sure. He was a very dislikeable person to say the least, so it wouldn't be a surprise to me if we were just victims of their dislike for Paul. For some people, it is easy to hate children. It was easy for them to disregard us as people. We were not made to feel welcome.

Out of them, there was one family member that we already knew, as he had visited us in Blackwell. That was Paul's younger brother, Kirby. "Uncle Kirby" was a tall, slender, military-type man with a militaristic personality. I'm not sure if he was actually in the military, but I assumed he was because of his appearance and all that we were told about him. We had initially met Kirby when Ralph and I were thirteen and fourteen years old, leaning more towards adulthood and away from being bratty kids, and unlike the rest of them, Kirby was nice to us.

I'm sure that, by now, you know Sarah well enough to realize that one can never be sure what she might do, but be confident that, whatever it is she does choose to do, it won't make any logical sense. This is another one of those things. Somehow, while we were at the reunion, Sarah made arrangements for Ralph to leave with Kirby on a vacation to Florida! So, from Arkansas, where we were already at a reunion with people we didn't know, my brother left for Florida with Kirby, and we went back to Blackwell . . . and packed up our house!

What the fuck just happened? What has she done? I wasn't allowed to know anything about what was happening, not old enough to be included in the adult conversations. Laughable, right? What kind of sense does that make? Sarah had purposefully placed me in so many situations that I should NEVER have been a part of, but I wasn't grown up enough to be included in discussions about what was about to happen in our lives. Fucking, Sarah. You kill me.

My stepdad Paul, Sarah, my youngest two siblings, and I packed our entire house and moved to Arkansas without my brother Ralph. He had zero idea what was happening when he was gone. Nobody told him shit either. On June 21, 1995, we packed the contents of our home into our vehicle and hit the road. I remember the exact date because it happened to be my fifteenth birthday. Sarah had given me a twenty-dollar bill for my gift, but Paul got upset, saying we needed all the money we had for travel, and made me give it back.

That was the day I left Blackwell, the place where I was born and the place I connect most strongly with my sexual assault as a child, the place that turns my stomach each time I have to go back for one reason or another. I left it. I left Mel and Johnnie. I left in that vehicle, crammed full of all our shit, my younger siblings, and two ignorant adults . . . and without my brother. When Sarah packed Ralph's room, she ripped his pictures from the walls without removing the tape or thumbtacks that held them in place, the corners ripping off because she didn't care enough to try and be the least bit careful. I know that they were only posters, papers on the wall, but we were so poor that we had nothing, so we really cherished our little things. Things mattered to us, and his private things mattered to him, but that bitch tore his posters down like she tore our lives apart.

Ralph didn't know that he would never see his friends again after that. He didn't know that he wasn't returning to Blackwell but to a whole new world. I think it was probably a week or so later that I saw Ralph again. We had moved to Cave City, Arkansas, into a rathole of an apartment in an apartment square with a huge, square, gravel parking space directly in the center. The entry sign read "Kings Apartments."

Kirby Archer brought my brother home, and we attended school at Cave City for just a short time, though we managed to make a friend or two. There was Angela, whose dad was a minister of some sort. That didn't matter though because she always had the best weed. Angela, Ralph, and I would smoke after lunch outside the school. Good times.

I was fifteen years old when I met Tonya, who quickly introduced me to her older brother, Shannon Beasley, who had just recently turned eighteen. Tonya liked Ralph, but Ralph didn't like her back. She was young and feisty, so she was kind of mean to him, often punching him in the arm and laughing about it. I never understood why she'd expect him to like being hit all the time. Nobody would like that. Tonya was also bigger than us, even though she was younger. Ralph and I were skinny bags of bones.

Tonya was around a lot, but she didn't live in our apartment square. She lived with her mom just a short distance away. Shannon did live in our square though, with his dad, Johnny. Shannon and I ended up getting together, and he became my boyfriend shortly after we moved in just a couple of apartments down from his.

Shannon wasn't a big guy by any means. Even at eighteen, he was very short. Maybe five foot three and a hundred and thirty pounds at most. He had long, stringy brown hair that hung out from the bottom of his ballcap and a super thick, ridiculous hillbilly accent that got even thicker the more whiskey he drank. The first thing I learned about Shannon, as his new girlfriend, was that he was meaner than fuck. He liked to drink whiskey from the bottle, and to put the icing on the cake, he was also a meth user. On top of that, he had a baby girl that wasn't yet a year old, the mother of whom he claimed had broken up with him.

At eighteen, he was already completely out of control, but being who I was at that time, I was a glutton for punishment and none of this scared me off. His ex, Tanya, was also young and wild—just as wild as Shannon—and with that connection, they had made a baby and become teenaged parents. Tanya popped in and out occasionally, which was how I got to know the baby.

What I didn't know was that its parents were still having sex. I was so stupid. Honestly, I didn't care much at all though. It was just another something for me to shrug my shoulders at.

I was fifteen years old at that point and equally wild and crazy. My mind wasn't anywhere near peaceful. I knew nothing of calmness or serenity. Shannon and I were like fire and gasoline, but we latched onto each other, and it became what it was.

My family didn't stay in Cave City long before we left Kings Apartments and moved a couple miles down the road to yet another roadside Arkansas town. We moved into a house that was literally sitting on the side of the highway out in the middle of nowhere. Paul's own parents lived directly across the highway from us in a large, fancy, brand-new home. They didn't bother with Ralph or me at all. It was openly acknowledged that we weren't welcome in their home, so we stayed away from them and them from us. Problem solved.

Uncle Kirby would visit us at our house when he was home from the military. He would come upstairs, where Ralph and my rooms were, and hang out up there with us, giving us cigarettes to smoke. Kirby liked to be alone with me too. Of course. Whatever. I wasn't shocked or hurt or confused about what was going on. I knew what I was supposed to do. One time he got me outside of his uncle's trailer house while it rained on us. He said it was romantic. Another time that was far less "romantic" was when he took me for a drive. (Still, nobody was asking questions about what was going on.)

I was in the passenger seat, well aware of what this drive was going to lead to. Kirby parked the car, climbed on top of me, and wasted no time engaging in adult sex with me—well, Kirby was an adult, and I was fifteen years old. He was sweating all over me, and I had no choice but to lay under him and accept what he was doing. When Kirby climaxed, he looked down at my face and said, "One's enough." Then he climbed off.

He took me back to join everyone else without a word and without any questions from Sarah. Like I said though, I didn't feel harmed. I just knew what to do. I don't guess I minded my job much by that point. *Just do it and be quiet*. I needed attention, and Kirby gave me his attention whenever he came around. I don't remember the last time I saw Kirby in person. But one day, after we left Arkansas, Ralph came to me with a story—a story you can read yourself if you Google search "Kirby Logan Archer."

On October 14, 2008, Kirby was given five consecutive life sentences for murder, kidnapping, robbery, and hijacking while running from authorities to avoid penalties for child molestation, as well as a slew of charges coming out of Arkansas. You might ask, "How was he caught?"

Nope. It wasn't me who turned him in. And Sarah would never be so brave as to call the police to protect me, assuming she even somehow decided she cared enough to want to. Luckily, another woman *did* defend her precious child and told authorities what a monster he was.

Uncle Kirby Archer, who had come into our lives around 1994 or 1995, the one who took my brother to Florida for countless days with my mother's blessing, is now serving life sentences for being a rapist and killer. I can fully assure you that, even after all of this information came to light, Sarah never bothered to open her shitty mouth to ask us if there was anything that we needed to tell her about our alone time with Kirby Archer. Not one damn time. Not one word out. Spineless.

She found out about all the charges when his story hit the news, and was well aware of what he was being accused of, and still never came to me and asked any sort of questions about the times we'd gone for drives or about him being alone with me in my room. And she sure as fuck never found the courage to ask my brother about his trip to Florida. When we got older into adulthood, I finally did bring myself to talk to Ralph about Kirby.

That is our own conversation though and won't be shared here. To this day, Sarah still hasn't been mother enough to bring it up. She is not brave enough to ask us anything.

I don't think I've mentioned it yet, but periodically, when Sarah thought I was being too much, she'd send off me to Robert H., the guy she was married to when I was born and the one she tried to make me believe was my father. Well, she pulled that shit on me again right about that same time. Of course, I was being blamed for being the bad one causing all the problems in the house. They were really caused by stepdad Paul, but because I was an out-of-control asshole kid (we all know why), I got the blame for all the disturbances. The guy was constantly putting me down. I couldn't do anything right by him. Any time my name came out of his mouth, he was bitching about me being there. I was like, "Hello? I fucking live here too! As a matter of fact, I was here first!"

One day, it became violent between the two of us. He had emotionally abused me so much that on that day I lost my self-control again. I lost my mind. I was so sick of Paul telling me to my face how much of a nuisance I was and how many problems I caused for Sarah. It wasn't Sarah telling me this, just her spokes-person. Anyway, I grabbed a handful of kitchen knives and threw them at Paul, one at a time. I know it's not funny by any means, and thankfully I was young and had terrible aim. It helped that it was colder outside, and Paul was wearing a pair of thick brown overalls that would have protected him from anything that came from me. Still, I can't imagine what would have happened to me if I had done any damage to that guy.

So, because of shit like that, I got sent to Robert H., who lived in Kirbyville, Missouri. You know, so he could teach me to be a good kid. I didn't have to stay long though, because Sarah had a plan worked out for me. This plan of hers was supposed to be to the benefit of both of us. (Right.) The plan would make things better for her and her marriage with Paul, and life would be better for me as well because I would be free from Paul and his abusive behavior towards me. Thanks, Sarah.

You see, just because I had moved away from Shannon doesn't mean that we had broken up. No, no. We were still crazy for each other all the time. Every chance he got, he drove over to see me. Shannon was a complete and total asshole jerk, but I still wanted him, and he still wanted me. Go figure. With Sarah's plan firmly in place, I was brought back from Kirbyville, and on August 16, 1996, eight weeks after my sixteenth birthday, Sarah drove Shannon and myself to the local courthouse where she signed paperwork that allowed me to marry Shannon Beasley.

I was fucking sixteen years old. I'm not exactly sure how this was supposed to benefit me at all, but I legally became a teenage bride, marrying Shannon later that afternoon in a trailer house in Poughkeepsie, Arkansas. The only people in attendance were the minister and his wife—who were completely thrilled to marry such a young couple—and a female cousin of Shannon's who was to be a witness. Sarah was not there. When we had left the courthouse that morning, with me standing right there, Sarah had looked at Shannon and said to him, "She's your problem now." Then she left me there.

My mother was gone, and I became a sixteen-year-old bride. *What the fuck am I supposed to do now?* I was officially on my own. I didn't have much to my name. No property and not even a lot of clothing to take with me into the marriage. I basically had a bag of stuff. I had no money, and since eighteen-year-old Shannon became my legal guardian that day, I was stuck following him around. Lucky me.

Chapter 6

I am a bit fuzzy about this portion of the timeline, but I do know that a short time after I was married off to Shannon, KD came from Oklahoma to Arkansas and took my younger siblings from Sarah and Paul. After all, KD was their biological father. I'm almost certain that Sarah didn't fight too hard, and Paul was more than eager to be rid of them. He wanted Sarah all to himself, without her children in the way, and he was doing a good job at getting what he wanted.

DJ and Sandra were roughly eight and nine at the time. The two of them are about as close in age as Ralph and me. After my young siblings were out, that left only Ralph there to deal with Sarah and Paul. From the bottom of my heart, I can never be sorry enough for the way things turned out. I never thought for one moment that I would be separated from my siblings. I would have stayed if I could . . . to fight with them against the piece of garbage adults who put them through so much.

KD had the kids back with him in Oklahoma with his new wife, and from what I understand, she hated my siblings, so they had to go through their own hell, of which I know very little.

Maybe for the best. Ralph was with Sarah and Paul, and I was out there in the world with Shannon.

In 1996, I would have been in the nineth grade if not for the wedding—my second year of nineth grade actually—having completed my eighth-grade year at either Blackwell or Ponca City. We were back and forth between the two towns so much that it's hard to keep track. My first year of nineth grade was when shit went south for me and Beverly. Because of the violent nature of the fight, I'd been expelled and failed the year. The crazy thing is that, even though I was a "bad kid" or whatever, I was super smart. I made A's and B's on my report cards, even though I never was one for actually studying. So much for that though.

After we married, Shannon and I stayed with his mom and stepdad mostly. We did stay sometimes with other members of his family, but like I said already, Shannon was an asshole, so even his relatives didn't want him hanging around if they had any sense. And now it wasn't only Shannon but his a sixteen-year-old asshole wife following him around as well.

I didn't own a car or have a driver's license, and I wasn't allowed to leave and go places without Shannon, so the both of us enrolled into a Vo-Tech school locally. I could do that because I was now a wife and legally an adult. No more public school for me, and so Vo-Tech it was. Shannon and I attended classes there for just a couple of weeks when I took the test to obtain my high school diploma and passed. This was in 1996. Looking back, I have no idea how I was able to do that. I'd barely made it through eighth grade (due to circumstances), and nineth had been a no-go twice.

My brain was not even close to processing as it should, yet I still somehow passed that damn test for my GED class and didn't have to attend anymore. Which meant that Shannon didn't need to attend anymore either. Not because he had passed his own test, but because he had only gone at all so that he could keep an eye on me. He needed to make sure that I wasn't talking to other boys while I was out of his sight. Shannon was paranoid that I'd find someone else to talk to besides him, and he couldn't have that. I was pretty happy when my diploma came in the mail. I even called Sarah and told her of my accomplishment.

Shannon's mom, Willy B., was so good to me. I honestly mean that. Her name is actually Wilene, but she always allowed me to call her Willy B., which still makes me smile. I started because I had heard someone else call her by that same name, and she never made me stop. I could tell Willy B. cared for me. All the time that Shannon and I stayed with her, she took care of me. I kept her house clean for her, and she taught me stuff like how to make potato salad. She treated me like a daughter, and I loved that feeling. I could tell that she was thankful to have someone cleaning in the home, because not everyone did. Her house was like a revolving door for anyone in the family who couldn't make ends meet—mainly Shannon but others too.

She also stopped Shannon from beating me up all the time. As much as she could anyways. Shannon was exceptionally strong for someone so scrawny. His naturally violent temper was unreal, but if he had meth or whiskey in his system, he was beyond violent and beyond strong. She got in between us several times to stop him from getting to me. Thank you, Willy B.

Shannon and I were together for four years though, and I didn't always get to hide behind her. I was young with a violent temper and so was Shannon. Plus, like I said, he liked to drink whiskey and smoke meth with his hillbilly friends, which was an instant trigger for a violent fight. Being with Shannon is how I learned what meth was. I saw firsthand what it did to people while I was with him, and I knew for a fact that I didn't want any part of that. If I only made one smart decision in life up to that point, it was avoiding meth.

Shannon and I spent four years together fighting like cats and dogs, bitter enemies forced to live with each other. The first time I was ever hit in the face by a guy's fist, it was Shannon's. He beat me up with his fists, and I beat him back with mine. He'd pull my hair and sling me across the room by my own hair, and I'd scratch his face and neck to make him bloody. We beat each other like that constantly.

We worked together in the same place once. We got into some heated trouble with our boss because Shannon came close to beating me in the back of the restaurant. The customers in the front could hear us screaming and cussing. Shannon had me cornered and wouldn't let me go. Some co-worker buddies of ours finally convinced Shannon to let me loose. The next day, we were both confronted by Charlotte, our boss, who always had a lit cigarette in her hand. In 1996/1997, a person could still smoke inside diners. It's odd now to think about that ever being okay. Smoking inside a restaurant, I mean.

Another time, when I was pregnant with our only child, David, Shannon pelted me with rocks as I walked up the driveway. I had taken my dog for a walk and purposefully stayed gone a little longer. When Shannon saw me walking up the drive, he wasn't concerned for his pregnant bride. Instead, he was so angry with me for being gone so long that he threw those rocks at me from the driveway and cussed me while he did so. Shannon spread rumors and wasn't afraid to say to my face that he was sure that our baby would be born black because there was a black family who lived next door and had befriended me. So, of course, I must have been cheating on him with someone there. I didn't have a car and wasn't allowed to leave without Shannon, so obviously, I must have cheated with the neighbor. I hated Shannon. He humiliated me so much. There wasn't a time that he wasn't hammered on something and acting like a loud-ass moron.

Aside from the job we worked together at the restaurant, Shannon wasn't interested in keeping a job as he didn't like having one. He was able to make a little money going to work on occasional weekends at the animal-sale barns with his cousin Jerrod. That money didn't do me any good though. Shannon didn't put any effort into making a living, so he always made a bare minimum. After cigarettes, booze, and meth, that didn't leave much financial support for his teen bride. I had a couple of jobs those years when I was with Shannon, but it was hard to keep them long term because of Shannon. He was notorious for showing up at my work and getting me fired. We beat the shit out of each other so much that I always had a bruise showing someplace. He would come to my job and start fights with me in front of people—assuming he'd decided to let me out of the house that day to leave for work at all. I couldn't control Shannon from coming to my workplaces, so I usually became a liability and was let go. And all because Shannon was constantly high on meth and paranoid. Because Shannon couldn't control himself. *Good job, Sarah. This is really turning out well for me.* She may have made things easier for herself by giving me away to Shannon, but it didn't work out so well for me.

I started my journey with Shannon without a dime in my pocket and struggled to take care of myself, not because I'm not capable but because I belonged to someone who wasn't my teammate but my bully. He was selfish and didn't care who his destructive nature hurt. He still doesn't.

There was a short time after my son was born that we did manage to have our own place. Sarah came from Oklahoma to Arkansas to meet my firstborn child. She brought one of my siblings and his friend with her. While with us, Sarah witnessed Shannon and I get into a brutal fight. He couldn't keep his insane jealousy under wraps for even just that one day. Fucking Shannon. I swear. But Sarah still headed back for Oklahoma without me and my baby. Maybe she thought I was big enough to handle physical abuse all on my own. Whether I was or wasn't, I still had to do it without Sarah.

As I've said, Shannon and I beat each other up. Shannon hit me all the time in front of people, mainly his family members and his dopehead buddies. Willy B. was the only person who really stood up in concern for me. I think everyone else just tried to ignore it. Nobody wanted to deal with Shannon because he was an out-of-control, drunken dumb ass, and they thought I was just as stupid for being with him. Shannon did what Shannon wanted and would cuss anyone who tried to have any authority over him. Shannon would cuss his own parents. Shannon cussed people all the time. Shannon cussed me all the time, accompanied by a whole lot of pushing, shoving, and forcibly holding me down on the ground. I was his person. I belonged to him, so he was free (he thought) to do to me whatever he pleased, including sex.

I never wanted to have sex with Shannon because he was so mean and hateful to me all the time. For fuck sake, Shannon called me bitch more than he used my actual name. As I listened to Shannon cuss me, it just made me despise him more and more. I developed a coldness. All that said though, everything I was going through with Shannon was preparing me for my future, though I didn't know that yet.

At night, after a day full of fighting, Shannon wouldn't allow me to sleep on the bed. He wouldn't allow me to sleep on the couch either. He made me sleep on the floor next to the bed with no blanket. If I tried to fight my way back onto the bed, he'd punch me back off of it, and if I tried to leave the room, it would turn into a knockdown, drag-out fight. I just learned to sleep on the floor. If I had ever truly cared for Shannon in a way that was more than just lust, I no longer did. I was being cussed all day, and fighting or not, if Shannon wanted sex that night, he was going to use my body for what was good for him. No feeling involved or needed. Sometimes, I didn't even need to be awake when Shannon needed me for sex, and he sure as fuck didn't need or care about my permission.

Countless times I woke up to Shannon giving me oral sex, or just on top of my body trying to get himself inside without me being there mentally or emotionally. He just needed my vagina. It's amazing how someone so young could have the power to make me feel so worthless. I had already been in damage mode when I met Shannon, but he still got to have his own page in my book.

On July 24, 1998, one month and three days after I turned eighteen, I birthed my only child with Shannon: my first son, David. At eighteen, I was a new bride, a stepmother (though the child didn't live with us), a new mom, and I was scared. I was alone in Arkansas. I didn't have a mother, a dad, siblings, close friends, or anyone I could turn to. Willy B. seemed to be the only person who cared enough for me to hold me tightly. To this day, I am sure she doesn't know how much those hugs saved me. I used to thank her often, as a teen bride and young mother, but still . . . all of these years later, I don't think it was enough. I know it was her that kept me alive during that time in my life. Thank you, Willy B., for loving me.

* * *

After I birthed David, I was desperate to get away from Shannon. For some reason, it was okay in my mind that Shannon was hitting me, but I didn't want him to hurt my baby, which is exactly what was starting to happen. It started the very day David was born. That afternoon, Shannon's drunk self showed up to the hospital and was loud and disrespectful on the unit, where he bumped into one of his neanderthal buddies, who just happened to be there waiting for his own child to be born. They got into trouble with the nursing staff because they were racing IV poles down the hallway and laughing loudly over it. It was like they were children on the playground, not fathers waiting for their gifts from the birthing unit. Shannon and his stupid friend were made to leave.

Our homelife was no different after David was born. Shannon liked to drink, and he liked to fight with me when he was drunk. It didn't matter to him if we had a baby or not. I watched Shannon fall with my baby in his arms once because he was drunk and missed a step. He and my son both landed on the ground.

Countless times I picked up my son to find him smelling of alcohol because of Shannon. Holding the baby in my arms didn't stop me from being hit either. So many times, I held on tightly to my son to stop Shannon from taking him away while I was being punched to let go. I also fought to get David out of Shannon's arms while he was drunk and crazy. David cried so much, scared and confused as to what was happening. He was caught in the middle while a crazy, out-of-control, drunk father and a young desperate mother physically fought over his body.

I am sorry that happened, David. I never wanted to put a baby in a situation like that. I didn't know that I would have to fight to keep my firstborn son from harm. I had hoped Shannon would be good, but hope was never enough. He was a maniac and will be as long as he lives. I'm sorry, David, for not giving you a better father.

I did run away from Shannon a couple of times, but each time, I made my way back because . . . well, I just didn't have a clue what to do. Each time, someone went out of their way to load up myself and my baby so that we could get away and be free from violent Shannon . . . and I just went back. That must've been so frustrating for those who did try to help us. I'm so sorry to those people as well. Thank you for going out of your way to be good people.

The last time I left Shannon though, I knew for a fact that I wouldn't be back. That time, I was prepared. There wasn't one thing about me that Shannon paid real attention to. Shannon didn't know anything about what I had in my dresser drawers, so he never noticed a thing when I began to pack away my clothing. If I had any cash to my name, Shannon made sure it was his cash, so I started hiding money in the picture frames on the walls. He never knew. I took care of the baby. Shannon didn't know what David had and what he didn't. Shannon didn't notice when so many of our things disappeared from the house and were stashed in a neighbor's shed close by. In May 1999, Shannon came home from working the sale barns to find me and my ten-month-old baby gone from the house.

After we left that time, Shannon never tried to get me to return. He acted as if David and I had dropped off of the face of the planet, and it wasn't long before I heard that he was having children with another woman, named Crystal. She was a childhood friend to Tonya, his younger sister, so she was younger than Shannon and me. Man, did I feel bad for her. They didn't stay together very long either, only long enough for her to birth two more of his children. She realized super early what a sack of garbage that guy was and took her two beautiful children, raising them without the negative influence of Shannon. They turned out so good those two kids. I'm so proud of them, and of you, Crystal. You are an amazing mom.

I don't really blame Shannon for what happened when the both of us were still kids. Yes, some of his anger and violent nature towards me wasn't needed and could have been avoided. Shannon didn't have to be so mean to me. After all, most of us have the capability to make adult decisions after the brain reaches a certain level of maturity—like being able to use self-control, for example. If I say these things about Shannon though, then maybe I need to say them about myself, because I was violent as well. Self-control wasn't within either of our capabilities—willing capabilities at least.

I was violent because all I knew was fight or flight. I didn't know at that time that was what I was experiencing, but now that I'm older, with years of mental-health help under my belt, I get it. Coming from trauma, even before Shannon, my young mind had already been wired into fight mode. The choice to fight or run away to save myself was all I knew. That was the way of it for me in every instance. I knew nothing at all about how to have a regular constructive conversation. I only knew how to fight, scream, cuss, yell, hit, or run away.

It was the same for Shannon but worse. By "worse", I mean that he added crazy mind-altering substances to his already mentally ill self and made it worse for both of us. From what I understand, Shannon used to watch violent episodes happen between his own parents, with his father being the aggressor. From watching this violent behavior, as well as experiencing physical trauma, Shannon made whiskey and meth his escape from reality and his crutch to lean on—a crutch that he used as an excuse to be a violently crazed person . . . a cancer on the face of society.

I think Shannon could have changed if he really would have tried, but he never wanted to be a good human. Not once did he ever make an effort to be a productive member of our community or our family. We were two very violent young adults living as man and wife and taking every ounce of aggression out on each other in beatings. There is no way in that moment of our lives that any amount of mental-help therapy would have helped us. We were both just crazy. Two crazy people can't raise a good kid. At least I had enough sense to think about David.

Chapter 7

When I left the state of Arkansas with my baby, we made our way to Arkansas City, Kansas. "Ark. City" for short. David and I moved to Kansas because that's where Sarah was, and sadly, she was the only other person I had. At that time, I suppose I was still searching for a mother within Sarah, the woman who had left me broken hearted and disappointed countless times, but I was also a female who'd just freed herself from a violently abusive marriage. I just needed my mom—or what there was of her available to me. Even after everything from before, I had put it behind me and tried to go to her again.

When I got to Ark. City in 1999, Sarah and KD were living together again as man and wife. Holy shit! The details? I don't think any of us want to know how they ended back together, but they did. (Some of my years run together, and some things I missed out on because I was consumed by Shannon.) I know that, before David was born (so roughly 1997), Shannon and I had visited Sarah, Paul, and Ralph in Pryor, Oklahoma. They lived in a small trailer house, and Sarah worked in the café down the street. I don't remember what Paul did for work, but I remember specifically that my brother was made to bus tables, not because they wanted to teach him the importance of savings, but because they wanted his income to "help pay bills." The moment Paul and Sarah had my brother to themselves, they figured they had a servant, and that's exactly how he was treated. Then, by the end of 1998, Sarah and Paul had split up, and she was back with KD and living in Ark. City.

Shannon and I, still married at the time, later traveled with our son to Kansas so we could watch Ralph graduate high school. It was while I was there in 1998 that I saw Johnnie for the first time since I was a girl, the day he'd left me in Blackwell "for a job" and didn't come back for me. It was hard for me to sit there, look at Johnnie, and know that I had been so emotionally attached to a grown man when I was a fourteen-year-old girl. I had really thought that I was in love with Johnnie. He'd made me believe he was someone he wasn't. He had never been my boyfriend, as he was a married man, but he was my only friend. In my heart, I'd really believed that, but in his heart, I was just some stupid kid that he was able to use.

Shannon was there with me. If he had known that there had ever been something between Johnnie and me, he would've acted so incredibly stupid. He would have acted like an asshole. Not in my defense but out of jealousy—a jealousy that there would have been zero reason for and would have been taken out on me. Nobody brought it up for that reason. We didn't want Shannon to ruin my brother's day by acting like a damn fool.

For me, it was the most completely awkward situation. Johnnie and I spoke a few words but nothing much. I remember just looking at him, feeling that something was off, but still not really realizing that what had been happening back then was rape. He'd been committing acts of perverse violence against me. I hadn't known it was wrong because my mother hadn't told me that it was wrong. As a matter of fact, she'd done nothing to stop it. That woman had facilitated my sexual assault. My own mother. Johnnie had never been my friend, and what he'd been doing wasn't loving me. It took me a very long time to figure that out. I was well into adulthood before I was able to come to that realization.

It's crazy what can happen to a child's brain when it's been traumatized for so many years. Something that a normal brain knows to be wrong, a brain like mine doesn't; confused at the line between right and wrong. For years to come, I allowed myself to accept damaging behavior, letting it ruin my mental and physical state all because abuse was made a normalcy beginning at childhood. For some of us, being normal isn't a possibility. Why didn't I just tell someone? Why didn't I tell a teacher or the police or someone else's parents that, for years, I had been being assaulted by men? Well . . . why would I? How did I know it was wrong if it was normal? What was there to tell? When I got old enough to talk, why didn't I tell someone what had happened with Alvie? I remembered it. I thought about it. Why didn't I say it out loud? (Or did I maybe . . . but nobody cared?) I'll tell you why. It's because I had been groomed.

The adults had succeeded in using me to lash out at, hit, and molest, and I just took it. I had learned to accept it. Every one of them—even Sarah, who still had some sort of bungy-type hold on me at the time—had done her part in my grooming process. She'd tried to turn me into something that I most definitely was not. And even in 1999, when I went back to live with her and KD, they were trying their best to suck me back in.

Living back with Sarah allowed Johnnie to make his way back around. He wanted another go at me. He wanted one last shot at fucking with my mind and my body. I was nineteen and Johnnie had to be thirty or close to it when me had me back on the floor of my bedroom, telling me disgusting things in order to get my pants off. I lay there with him, shaky and unsure of the moment. I knew that I didn't want to be there, but I still didn't know how to say no. After what seemed like an hour of me avoiding his advances, Sarah finally came up the stairs and opened my bedroom door. Johnnie looked up at Sarah from the floor and said, "She doesn't want to have sex." Sarah shrugged her shoulders like she had done so many times before and walked away. Johnnie also got up then and left. (I only saw Johnnie once more after that day, when I walked into a house in Ponca, and there he sat. We didn't speak.)

It was 2016 or 2017 when Ralph got in touch with me and told me that Johnnie was dead. It sounded like someone had gotten him a bad bag of dope, because he shot it into his veins and died. The very next day, one of his sisters—not the rapist sister but another—did dope out of the exact same bag and died as well. True story.

After hearing the news about Johnnie, I wasn't sure how I felt. I should have felt relief, but that wasn't it. Maybe I was in shock because there wasn't any disbelief. Just like so many other things in my life, it was just something that happened, though I did shed a tear. I will never see him ever again in life. My current husband and I traveled to Blackwell for the funeral with my brother Ralph. I knew that I was there for Johnnie's funeral, but I kept thinking, *Where's Mel? Where's the pedophile who raped me in the silence of my own prison?* That's where my mind was. Was he there too? In the same building I was? I just knew he would be. Mel and Johnnie—those two sorry wastes of life—were a child-molesting team.

My heart was about to burst out of my chest with anxiety, thinking I'd see Mel that day. I practiced what I would say to him, though not out loud of course. Mel wasn't there though. It soon became clear as a bell to me why he didn't attend his best friend's funeral. Johnnies' sister—the scum bitch who put her hands on my brother—let me know that Mel had even had his way with her own young daughter. The niece of Mel's child-molesting cohort had fallen victim as well. She was upset, telling me her daughter suffered from nightmares and anxiety because of Mel. I was very sorry for her and her daughter. That was the last day I saw her as well.

Anyway, as I've said, by 1999, Sarah and KD were reunited and living together with the kids and Ralph in Ark. City, while I was making my way from Arkansas to Kansas. I tell you, nothing had changed. It was like opening the door back into my childhood. Ralph and I didn't stay in that house for long. Only as long as we absolutely had to.

My question was why in the fuck those two got back together. Why did Sarah do it? After he'd made it perfectly clear to Sarah that he wanted to have sex with her daughter, why did she think that it was safe to get back with the guy? Did she not remember that whole "asking for a threesome" thing? Then again, I guess maybe I do know why: because he had her two youngest kids. Paul had divorced her, and she wasn't a strong enough person to be on her own. Sarah is co-dependent. She can't be the leader. KD no longer had a wife either, so it only made sense for her. I could only roll my eyes at the sight of them there together. So pathetic.

When I arrived in Ark. City, Ralph quickly got me hired on at the restaurant/steakhouse where he worked. A lot of young people worked there, and it was fun for me to be around new people close to my own age. Being Ralph's sister helped a lot. Everyone liked Ralph. What was there not to like? The guy is literally my best friend. So, because everyone was really in with Ralph, it made it easier for me to be accepted, which was something that had never been easy for me in the past. I know that I wouldn't have been accepted by people so easily if it wasn't for Ralph. By that point, I had developed a social anxiety disorder. I was kind of mean and was super on-edge all the time. People who got to know me dubbed me "Ralph's crazy sister." It still isn't easy for me to make friends actually. In any case, I know how difficult it would have been for me then if it hadn't been for Ralph having my back. I love my brother.

As soon as we could, Ralph and I moved out of Sarah's house with my baby. We only moved a couple of blocks away, but it was far enough! Having our own place was great. We went halves on everything. Well . . . mostly. Once again, Ralph would often come to my rescue, picking up slack for me a lot. I was irresponsible with money, on top of having a toddler to provide for. We worked all day and hung out all night. At eighteen and nineteen years old, we had jobs, our own house, and a car, which was more than some of our buddies had. So, it was okay for the buddies to hang out at our place. We liked having company, and even though I was the only parent among our circle, nobody minded that I had a toddler.

Everyone in our group was good to David, occasionally even taking David out to play while I was able to rest. I appreciated that so much, but that doesn't mean I wasn't irresponsible in my role as a mom. I was young and stupid. I smoked cigarettes in the same house as my child and allowed others to do so as well. We had mice in the kitchen, but I didn't do a lot to deal with the issue aside from setting out traps and cleaning up. But we still had mice.

I worked, hung out, did irresponsible shit, and had my little boy on my hip as often as time allowed. I didn't want other people to have to take care of David, so I kept him with me even when he probably shouldn't have been. I was his mom. Ralph and I did well. We made a good team for being so young, but then again, we'd always been a good team.

One of our buddies, John Zelman, used to spend time with David when I couldn't get a sitter and had to be at work. John and I had begun to become somewhat close just around the time that he left Ark. City and moved to Bartlesville, Oklahoma. That was where his own father was. Sadly, with me being me and full of bad decision-making, I eventually followed John Zelman to Bartlesville. Ralph was so upset with me. I was so selfish that I didn't consider Ralph's feelings or what kind of financial bind I would leave him in, which I really did. When I left, I never even told anyone. I just gathered up David and left, leaving my brother responsible for everything on his own. I wasn't a good sister to Ralph. He was the much better teammate. I'm sorry, Ralph.

David and I stayed with John and his dad, though it was the shortest-lived stay of them all. I got employment at a place called The Golden Coral. I didn't have much work experience except as kitchen staff, so that's what I did. I worked inside the bakery portion of this buffet-type restaurant. It was in that Golden Coral, in early 2000, that I met Mike Walker.

Mike and I locked eyes, and the flirting began instantly. We more than hit it off. It was so noticeable that we were separated into different areas of the building by management because we wouldn't get anything done. All we did was play around with each other like little kids. That is ultimately the reason my stay with John ended so quickly. Of course, Mike said that my son and I could stay with him and his mom, Cindy. Mike was also nineteen and had a son of his own, a toddler seven months older than David. He too was a single parent. Immediately, it seemed like Mike and I were a match. After a whirlwind of a week in Bartlesville, I moved my son and I in with Mike, his son (Mike Jr.), and Mike's mom, Cindy. I know it was the end of May 2000, because I spent my twentieth birthday with Mike Walker—which would be followed by nine more birthdays, all shitty, that I would spend with him.

I told you that those years were full of bad decision-making—bad decisions that would include my sex life. Mike and I didn't use protection the first time we had sex, which happened within days of us meeting while I was technically still living at John's. As cute as I thought Mike was, and as hot as we were for each other, that doesn't mean that our first time was either cute or hot. It wasn't. I should have actually found it scary and alarming. It started out just fine. We were in his room at his mom's house, having sex under blankets, when his house phone rang.

That's when what should have been my first red flag with Mike happened. I'm sure that, deep in the back of my abnormal brain, it probably was . . . but being me, it didn't scare me as much as it should have. When Mike's house phone rang, instead of him letting anyone else pick it up—you know, because he was right in the middle of something—he got up to answer the phone. Then I listened and watched as Mike raged at the person on the other end of the line, cussing and screaming right in front of me. I should have been shocked, but I wasn't. Like I said, it didn't bother me as much as it should have. When the rage call was over, Mike got back into bed with me, and we continued doing what we'd been in the middle of before the call. Like nothing had happened. As though he hadn't just screamed his head off five second before, he was able to continue having sex without skipping a beat. Apparently, I wasn't worried about myself or my son at that moment.

I asked a question earlier: What was Sarah thinking when she got together with KD? In my later years, I've had to ask myself that exact same question. My only answer is that it wasn't because I was stupid. I didn't know what to look for in a man or a relationship. And I didn't know anything about who God was at the time. Sarah certainly hadn't done her best teaching us—so he wasn't a role model for me. I was stupid, irresponsible, and uneducated. That was my answer for me, but I can't answer for Sarah. I was just stupid. I was alone. I wanted a companion. And I was young and wanted to have sex. I wanted to somehow have a family. I wanted a strong man to raise sons with and lead our family. I wanted normalcy. Nothing about Mike and I turned out to be normal. I told you already that I was clueless as to what was really important in looking for a partner and what matters in a relationship, so I just followed my eyes, my lustful nature, and of course, my good ole "bad at making good decisions" brain. That day, I should have taken my son and never returned. That isn't what I did though. I stayed around, moved in, and became part of "Mike Walker World."

The person on the other end of the phone line that first day with Mike was called Crickett. Yes, that was her real birth name. Crickett was mother to Mike's two-year-old son who lived with him. As it turns out, shortly before I showed up—like "within that same week"—Crickett had been living there in the house with everyone else. One morning, Mike woke up to find Crickett gone. She'd left the house the night before while everyone was sleeping and got on a bus for California, which was where they'd all come from. And she'd left without Mike Jr.

Of course, the screaming fit I'd witnessed that first night was directed at the mother of his child, calling her names, blaming her for giving him a child that he hadn't asked for, and then running off and leaving them. Cussing, he called her the worst mother on the planet and screamed about how she would never see her son again. As I'd watched Mike in that moment and listened to his display of anger, I'd thought to myself, *What kind of mother leaves her baby in the middle of the night?* I didn't know Crickett, and I was judging her for being a terrible mom. I couldn't believe how selfish it was of her to leave her son behind just because she didn't want to be a mother any longer. At least, that's what Mike managed to convince me of in just a single day.

On that first day when we were sexually active with each other, he was able to fully convince me that she was the bad guy, and he was the loving father who provided not only for them but his own mother as well. Even after I had just witnessed him in such a vulgar moment, jumping around, yelling and cussing her like she was the enemy, I was still critical of her. Wow, huh?

Not too smart on my part, staying around and watching that, but there was still something about Mike that had my attention and made me want to stay. Not once did I think about David being in harm's way, at least at first. Mike was already father to a boy, so surely, he would love my son too.

That was May of 2000. On June 21, 2000, I turned twenty. For the life of me, I can't believe that I actually made it to that age. I still can't believe that, by that point of my life, I hadn't been lost, killed, or kidnapped. As much shit as my little frame had been through, I was amazed to be alive. That was shocking to me, not violence.

There are plenty of times as a crazy kid I could have gotten myself seriously injured. One day when I was probably around thirteen—no older, at least, as I was still attending school—I was being heavily harassed and picked on by a boy, probably just for being ugly and poor. Of course, I was a firecracker of a kid. I cussed and had fistfights on a regular basis. I had to. It didn't matter to me who it was that was making me miserable, I was ready to snap back. This boy picked on me so much that, by the end of the school day, I had gone mad. I was so crazy by day's end that I marched my tiny, eighty-something-pound frame right to his older sister's apartment, though she was obviously way too old for me to be talking shit to. My loud self proceeded to tell her how much of an asshole her brother was, how he'd been so terrible to me all day, and how I wanted her to do something about it.

I was mean and loud and out of control. How could I not be? I had been bullied the entire day, and my emotions were very heightened. I didn't know one thing about how to control my anger. This teenaged/adult woman did not care for having me in her face yelling about how her bad brother was to me. To get to this older sister's apartment, I'd had to climb a flight of stairs. Getting back down them was quicker as she had wrapped her fingers through my long hair and thrown me. I was like that fucking ball inside a pinball machine. She threw me so hard that I just bounced off the walls of that narrow staircase all the way to the bottom. I probably could have gotten myself seriously hurt that day. Just like I could have been at all the adult campsite parties I attended before we moved to Arkansas and I was married off at sixteen. I shouldn't have been alone at those, drinking with adults.

Then there was the time when I was about thirteen and was supposed to be babysitting for Penny (Brenda's daughter), who was nineteen, but instead was drunk on Southern Comfort. That night, Penny and I entertained an old man with a strip dance, and when he was too drunk to notice, we stole his wallet, found his keys, and stole his truck. We continued with this dangerous behavior, and by the end of that same night, I was in trouble. I puked in "Cousin Jason's" backseat and was put out of the car onto the side of the road. When Penny woke me up, I was in a ditch covered in my own vomit. It was dark, pouring down rain, and I was being picked up and put into a car that was driven by someone I didn't know. They took us back to Penny's house, where we stayed. I probably could have died or been stolen off the side of the road that night.

As a girl, I used to spray hairspray into circles on my bedroom carpets, light it on fire, and then hurriedly put it out. I'm thankful I didn't set my house or family on fire. I was so stupid. Then there were all the times I didn't go to school and instead went with Johnnie to his buddy's house, where we'd smoke weed and stay all day. The list could go on and on. I am glad and grateful that I even made it through those dangerous situations to meet Mike, though he would only be the next thing I would have to survive.

Chapter 8

At twenty years old, I figured that (since I was an adult) I could take charge of my own life. Once again, I should have thought it through.

I stayed with Mike because I thought that I felt something for him. I thought that there was a connection. I even had it in my mind that, because I felt such a strong connection, Mike had to be my soulmate. Was he? Had I found a soulmate in Mike Walker? If so, he messed it up right away, but even with the ugly words, the rude gestures towards me, and the way he was so secretive about everything all the time, it was not enough to make me pack our stuff and move on.

There was this one time when I did have just an ounce of courage. Early in our relationship, I did fight back with Mike, and I tried to leave. I was pregnant with our son Jacob at the time. I took my son David by the hand, and we took off on foot. I didn't know where we were going, but we were leaving. It was then that Mike pulled up beside us as we walked down the road, grabbed David from me, put him into his car, and took off. Mike had me in that moment. I ran back to his house and begged for my son back. A normal brain, one not already traumatized, would have gone to the police. Instead, I ran back to Mike and pleaded with him.

He convinced me that we were already a family, and I'd be messing up the toddlers by leaving again. The real connection that I "just knew" I had with Mike was probably just my pregnancy. Our son Jacob was born in March of 2001. I'd met Mike in May of 2000 and birthed his son not even a year later. There I was, twenty years old, about to turn twenty-one in June, and I had become a mom to two toddlers and a brand-new baby.

That's right. I said two toddlers. The very second I moved into Mike's house, I became responsible for Mike Jr. Mike had found his son a replacement mom. And Mike let me know just about daily that I wasn't Mike Jr's "real mom." I looked after all his needs and cared for him physically like a real mom, but still Mike openly voiced the reality that even though Crickett could still come back, and Mike Jr. would want his real mom, I had to keep doing what I was doing until that happened. That was Mike's plan.

Mike Jr. also knew that I wasn't Crickett. The poor kid probably *did* want his real mom. I wanted him to have his real mom. He didn't like me or want me, and I could tell. I guess I kind of didn't like him either. I tried so hard, but with Mike letting me know up front that I wasn't the real mom, and then pointing out mistakes I was making daily with Mike Jr., it made it so difficult to bond with this new little boy I called "son." We both felt it, but Mike forced us all to be together. Nobody had a choice but Mike. Nobody's opinion mattered but Mike's. This was my new family.

While David and I were in the process of moving into Mike's house, Cindy's boyfriend Billy was also in the process of moving in. Cindy was older than Billy by a good twenty years. That age difference didn't matter to Billy in the least. It was obvious how much he cared for Cindy. He was so good to her, and she could be pretty mean to him if she wanted.

Cindy was in her early forties when we met. I'd say she was about five foot two, with thin, stringy, strawberry-colored hair. She was a bit overweight from living a life of drug and alcohol abuse. Cindy was a lady though, and even though she was a regular user of street drugs, she could still very much compose herself in a social setting. She had the gift of gab. I don't know a person who didn't like Cindy. I'm sure there were some, but none that I ever met. Maybe that charisma she carried, coupled with their mutual liking of meth, is why Billy stayed.

Billy was maybe a year or so older than me. He was tall and thin, with long brown hair that grew well down past his shoulders. Billy didn't have good teeth, but he had a good smile. I know that doesn't seem to make sense, but it was true. His smile could cheer up a bad day.

I liked Billy as a person. Again, even though he also was a meth user, he never seemed off. He was the same Billy all the time: a genuinely nice person. I was never scared of Billy, and I never worried over him. He was always good to me and David both. As a matter of fact, Cindy used to joke that she was gifting Billy to me in her will after she died. Aside from the meth part, Billy was a great human being with a wonderful soul. He was always happy, always did everything for the kids, making a big deal out of every holiday, and was an amazing dad even though none of the children belonged to him. He had the heart of a father. Billy was always happy except for when Cindy was coming down from a meth high, and then it was all bad for Billy.

I could tell that Cindy loved me, and she loved my kids so much. She was such a good grandmother, and it saddens me that my children won't have a life filled with their Gramma Cindy. Never once in the years we had together did she ever treat me crossly, and she went out of her way for her grandchildren every time it was possible. Her drug use never affected her demeanor towards us, but poor Billy . . . she'd let have it. I'm sure that, when she wasn't high, she still loved Billy, but she didn't know how to be sober. The first time I met my kids' Gramma Cindy, it was from behind closed doors. Mike had taken me to meet her before I moved in with them, but I had to talk to her through her bedroom door because she wouldn't open it. When I questioned Mike about why her lights were off, even though she was awake in there, he explained to me that she was in the dark with a flash-light trying to find a vein.

I knew what he was talking about because of my previous life with Shannon. I never saw Shannon using drugs via needle; I just saw the holes in his arms and then had to deal with him until and after he came down. When Cindy was coming down, it was the same deal for Billy. Cindy yelled at him a lot—constantly actually. She always called Billy a "son-of-a-bitch." She made him feel unworthy to the point that he would leave, though he never stayed away more than a couple of days at a time. It was always the same cycle. Every time. Cindy would be sad and cry to Mike because Billy had left, Mike would tell her in return what a bitch she was being, and she would agree and beg Billy to come back—and he always did. He always came back to bipolar Cindy and meth. It's strange to say that they honestly were a good couple when Cindy wasn't being hateful. She was so nice, the best lady in her heart, but when she wasn't, it was always Billy who suffered. Billy was always the same laid back, all-around nice guy whether he was high or sober. Always the same Billy.

The dynamic between Mike and his mom though . . . holy shit. I'd never witnessed a mother-son relationship as volatile as the one between them. Mike hated his mom. It was obvious. Mike hated all women actually, and his mom was no exception. Apparently coming from California, in the late seventies and early eighties, Cindy had lived a rough life. From the stories she used to tell me, some of that roughness was self-induced and some were the things she was made to do by drug cartel dudes.

The experiences behind those stories were at least part of the reason she'd had to let go of her two sons, Sonny Jr. and Mike, when they were just toddlers.

Sonny Jr. and Mike had spent a fair amount of time in foster care but were primarily raised by their father, Sonny Sr., who had not "spared the rod" with his sons. Sonny Sr. was also involved in the drug life and did not have a nurturing bone in his body. He was very brutal to his boys, mentally, physically, and emotionally. Mike told me stories of his father killing his favorite pets as punishment and cutting their beds in half with a chainsaw when he was high on drugs.

When the boys were just little, Sonny Sr. took a nineteen-year-old wife named Dina. Together, Sonny Sr. and Dina had three more children. Mike used to tell stories of his stepmom's abuse. Like how she would spoil the others with candy and purposefully leave him out. How she showered the others with affection but for him there was nothing but coldness. The same with food and toys. The three youngest children were allowed snacks and treats, with Sonny Jr. and Mike left with nothing but "wants." Mike would tell me these stories of his stepmom every time he was punishing me for what he thought was unfair treatment of his own son. I got to hear a lot of those stories.

Poor Cindy though. In Mike's eyes, everything that Mike had gone through as a child was her fault, and she would forever carry the blame for leaving him as a baby. Every day of our lives together, living in the same household, Mike made it hard for Cindy somehow. I can't tell you exactly how long Cindy had no contact with Mike, but I do know that when I met them, they had been living in the same house for more than a year. And I watched Cindy beg for Mike's forgiveness time and time again to no avail. I watched her shower Mike with love and affection. I watched her cry in embarrassment every time Mike would lay into her about how she was a bad mom, and he'd been left with his monster of a dad.

Mike refused to forgive Cindy. He rejected every offer she made to make things right. I firmly believe that this was why Cindy drank herself to death. Cindy drank vodka, and I know it was to drown the pain from her past shames, which Mike reminded her of daily. I watched her drink herself to death over the years. At the end of her life, she was bleeding internally from a lifetime of IV drug use and alcoholism. All her internal organs shut down, and she died the year she would have turned fifty. I miss Cindy all the time, but her pain wouldn't allow her to stay sober.

All of the fighting between Mike and Cindy was the reason we had to move out before Jacob was born. That, plus the fact that it was already a family of four adults and two toddlers and we were adding a baby. We needed more space. Me, Mike, and the toddlers got a house just across the bridge from Bartlesville in Dewey, Oklahoma. That was our home when I birthed Jacob, my second son. My little baby was so beautiful, with a head full of dark brown hair. That's not what Mike was expecting our boy to look like though. Mike is a Caucasian guy with peach-colored skin, strawberry-blond hair, and green eyes. Mike Jr. looks just like his father with all the same features. A small version of him. I, however, am a brown-skinned, brown-eyed, brown-haired Native American woman. Everything about me is brown. It was quite the shock for Mike to see that my Native DNA was so strong, and my blood ran thick in our baby.

He wasn't happy that Jacob didn't look like his blond brother, so he decided to give me grief over something that I had absolutely no control over. For such a long time, I had to listen to Mike doubting Jacob's paternity, and if it wasn't for the fact that his own father's bloodline came from Spain and had contributed to my son's dark hair, he would have insisted on genetic testing because I "probably cheated." I wasn't cheating on Mike, but it was what he believed and those are the words he used. What the fuck ever, Mike.

While we were living in that house in Dewey, I met Crickett for the first time. Mike Jr.'s "real mom." By this time, I had been in this for well over a year, taking care of Mike Jr. and adding another member to our family. On that day, Crickett had hopped a bus from California to Oklahoma and was suddenly sitting on the couch across the room. It was hard for me. I didn't like her, and I didn't even know her. The only thing I knew about this lady was every single word of trash that was ever said about her. In every conversation about Crickett, she was the bad guy. Mike told me that she knew he didn't want kids until he was twenty-five and had "tricked him" into getting her pregnant. Then one day, after deciding that she no longer wanted a family, she just left. Remember all that screaming over the phone?

So, there sat this girl. She hadn't shown herself in over a year, but she was in front of me now. After all this time that I had been taking bashings for not being a good enough mom for Mike Jr., even though I was trying to raise and love someone who didn't want me because he wanted his own mom instead. After all the days that I'd taken verbal and mental abuse meant for her but handed to me because I was there to receive it. After all the times I'd had to defend myself against Mike because I wasn't Crickett. Now she was sitting on my couch and talking about how good Mike looked and how he seemed to have come so far since she had left more than a year ago.

I wanted to choke the fucking life right out of her that day. I wanted to attack her. It was the first time I had ever met this absent mom in person, and I felt like I could rip her apart with my bare hands. Not because of who she was—the ex-girlfriend/baby momma—or what she had done by leaving her man behind. I hated her because I had taken every ounce of anger that both of these Mikes had for her. I'd absorbed every hateful word, every ugly look, every cold shoulder, every spout of anger and outburst that came from them because they were mad at her. Neither of those two liked me. Mike had me there because he needed someone to control, and like I said, Mike Jr. didn't want any mom but his own.

The energy was strong. Living with the anger that was meant for her fueled my anger at her. Was it her fault that I came into the picture so quickly after she left? Not at all. She left because she didn't want to be a victim to Mike's torment anymore. I get that 100 percent, but why not take your son with you? She left that baby, and he hated me for it. For that I had so much animosity. What I didn't know then was that Crickett hadn't just shown back up on her own. Mike had invited her to come to visit, and so she did. A day or so went by and then she was once again on a bus for California without her son.

Mike, our boys, and I stayed in Dewey for about a year, I guess. I was a young mother of two biological sons and a stepson who wished that I was his real mom, and a partner to a guy I had dreamt of escaping from since the first time I'd tried to leave. Damn, I wanted to get away from Mike so bad. The guy never stopped.

There was a time after Crickett had gotten back on the bus to California that I experienced some serious bullshit with Mike. Things weren't ever good between us, but anytime he thought he could fan the flames, he absolutely did. Mike liked to fight.

I'm not sure that people know this, but men can also get yeast infections. I don't know how Mike got one, but he did. Not a sexually transmitted disease but a yeast infection. Mike didn't know that he had a yeast infection until he finally went to a doctor and got a proper diagnosis. Instead, at the beginning of his symptoms, Mike took it upon himself to accuse me of giving him herpes, even though I didn't have herpes or any other

STD, nor have I ever had one surprisingly enough. He lost his damn mind, and he lost it at me, accusing me of cheating and being a whore (yada yada). He didn't stop there though. He then called every member of his family and told them that I gave him herpes. I didn't have herpes. Did Mike make any of those calls private? No. Every phone call was made right in front of me, so that each time, he could look me in the face and accuse me all over of doing something I didn't do.

The strangest of all these calls is the one he made to Crickett, telling her that she should go to the doctor and get checked because Lu had given him herpes. Lu. That was what Mike called me by. Why would he need to do that? Because (duh) he'd been having sex with Crickett when she'd come for that "visit" and then left again without Mike Jr. I must admit that it took me a couple of days to catch on to that one. All he'd ever done was talk about how much he hated her. I didn't know that he'd fuck her when she came back. I should have known right away, but by then I was already in Mike's clutches.

I'd been a part of his world so long that he had me exactly where he wanted me. Does anyone reading this know what the term "narcissist" means and how controlling a narcissistic person can be? A narcissist has the ability to consume a person and that's exactly what happened to me. From the moment I met Mike Walker, he started his own type of grooming process with me. Over the course of our entire relationship, he groomed me to be his slave, not only physically but mentally and emotionally as well, drilling into me that I was a bad mom, boring in bed, ghetto, ugly, and not his type . . . I was stupid and should think before I spoke. He'd call food I had prepared for him trash as he dropped it in the garbage can, grabbing his keys on the way out of the door to go and eat fast food while my kids and I sat there and ate my "garbage food." Cousin Anthony saw that happen firsthand. It was very much behavior that Mike found acceptable.

"How did I end up with an Indian?" Mike would ask me directly, as though he expected me to have an answer prepared for him. He'd make me sit on the bathroom floor while he was on the toilet. No matter how long it took. "You stay right there, Lu, just in case I need you. People die on the toilet, Lu." Mike didn't give a fuck about dying on the toilet. He wanted me right there like his puppet so he could keep an eye on me.

"You got my toothbrush, Lu?" I was responsible for getting him ready for his daily routine. Funny, huh? Not really. I told you that I was a slave to Mike, from actually putting the toothpaste on Mike's toothbrush to rubbing hemorrhoid cream around Mike's asshole. Of course, that was my fucking job. Inserting suppositories as well. Mike worked very hard every day "for our family," and so it was our fault he had hemorrhoids. "It's only right that you have to do it, Lu."

Anytime I thought that Mike might be in the wrong about anything, he was quickly able to manipulate me into thinking that whatever it was I was fussing about was all in my head, and that it wasn't him playing me for a damn dummy. When we argued about his call to Crickett, he weaseled his way out of it by letting me know that he wouldn't have had to make all those calls if I hadn't given him herpes in the first place. I know it doesn't make sense, but it's not supposed to. A narcissist doesn't use reason or logic or truth. They win by being loud, overbearing, manipulative, and violent.

I'm sure I don't need to tell you that, after his visit with a doctor and a proper diagnosis, he still didn't feel the need to apologize to me, even though he'd completely embarrassed and shamed me over and over with each of those explicit calls to friends and family. Mike doesn't have an apologetic bone in his body. He hurt my feelings so bad. I wasn't okay.

While we lived in Dewey and the boys were just toddlers, Mike was selling bricks of weed for the Mexicans. It was a little tense when they came, because there were always at least three of them, and they weren't there to be friends. These guys meant business. Mike knew a lot of people in the area, so he was able to sell those bricks of weed rather quickly. Mike was making these guys a lot of cash, and because he was making cash money, he was able to put some profit in his pocket, which made him very happy. His dealings with the Mexicans put us in danger, but it made Mike happy.

What Mike didn't like though, and what made him very unhappy, is that whenever the Mexicans came, he had to watch each of them kiss me on the cheek! They kissed my cheek on the way in, and again on the way out, every single time. I enjoyed the satisfaction way too much to be scared. I can't explain the happiness I got from those few seconds that fueled Mike's anger. He hated it so much, but what was he going to do?

Then one day, Mike said to me that we were looking for a new place to live because he didn't like Oklahoma anymore. I was never certain just why Mike wanted to leave so badly, but if I had to guess, it was something to do with his dealings. Are drug dealers honest? I got in touch with Robert H.—who Sarah was forever trying to convince me was my real father—who was living in Kirbyville, Missouri, with his wife, her son, and twin daughters. They allowed all of us to stay with them in Kirbyville while we prepared for a life in Missouri. Robert came to Oklahoma and helped us move our entire life to another state. I already knew what was waiting for us because of the times I had visited Robert H. and his wife Brenda as a kid. We eventually arrived at a mobile-home park in Kirbyville, Missouri. Set at the end of a two-way drive, there weren't many neighbors aside from the young couple across the way. Our entire stay was nothing less than awkward. Mike never made anything easy.

Robert and Brenda were a different type of people than Mike. They were more country backwoods type, and Mike was the outspoken asshole who complained about everything and never made any attempt to keep the peace. He wasn't concerned for how hard he made it for me or our kids, whom he left me to take care of while he hid in a room or outside someplace. Mike was also used to having weed in his pocket, which he didn't have access to yet because we were new to the area. Mike was mean as fuck already, but if he ran out of pot . . . all bad for Lu. Guess who got stuck with the verbal abuse because he needed someone to blame for his discomfort? I'd brought him to a state where he didn't know one person. I'd brought him to live in a trailer house that was full of dirty laundry, dirty dishes, and dog hair. I'd brought him to a place where he had no money and no connections.

All this verbal conflict, all this tension between adults, started the moment we arrived and continued until we left for our own place. Mike apparently didn't remember that he was the one who'd come to me and said that we MUST LEAVE OKLAHOMA! *Sigh.* Okay, Mike.

It wasn't long after meeting the young couple across the way that he once again knew a plethora of people, had pot connections, and was back to being his social-butterfly self. I didn't deserve any of that shit Mike dished out while we stayed in that trailer. I did nothing but try to stay as low key as possible while Mike left me in charge of all three children while he did as he pleased. He caused so much undeserved turmoil. Mike was in a new place, probably paranoid over whatever reason had caused us to leave Oklahoma in the first place, and was taking it out on me. I was trying to make things easier, but nothing was EVER easy with Mike. It didn't take long at all before we were able to move, but it seemed like forever.

Chapter 9

By the year 2002, we were residents of Blue Eye, Missouri. Blue Eye was just a tad north of the Arkansas/Missouri state border, so it was normal for people to commute across the dam to Branson. That is where all the jobs were. Branson, Missouri is a tourist town full of traffic, live-action theaters, attractions, shops, condo resorts, hotels, motels, and a variety of food options everywhere you looked. Anyone could find plenty of work there. I had been going to Branson since I was a kid because that's where Robert was primarily to be found. Whenever Sarah would get sick of me causing problems for her, she'd ship me off to Robert, which caused problems for me. It wasn't until after Robert died that I told Sarah this story:

Robert H., the guy who was supposed to be my "father," was married to a woman called Boogs when he tried to get me to lay naked with him in his bed. I was around eleven probably. His wife at the time had taken her own children on an outing, and they'd be gone for the day. It was after dinner, and I had gone upstairs on my way to the loft bathroom when I saw Robert lying on the upstairs bed, with the blankets up to his waist and naked as far as I could tell. Waiting. He gently tried to coax me into the bed with him. He wanted me under those blankets so he could touch me. Robert wanted to touch a child that day, one that was in his care. Caring for me wasn't in his mind at that moment. Instead, I became scared for my safety. I was in genuine fear for my body. Compared to me, a sixty-pound kid, Robert was a giant man. Every bit of six foot two and three hundred and fifty pounds. I was scared to death. Instead of climbing into that bed like he wanted, I locked myself in the bathroom where I stayed until I heard him get up and dressed. I listened to him walk down the stairs and out the door of the condo he shared with his wife and step-kids.

I never mentioned it to anyone until I started mental-health therapy, well into adulthood. I put it in my box of memories and never found the courage to confront him over it.

When Robert later married Brenda, who was large as well, she already had the twins. Visiting with them was terrible also. They had horrible eating habits. The kitchen always full of soda and snack boxes rather than real food. The freezer was full, but there was nothing you could prepare as a meal. Just precooked frozen items. Piles of laundry usually covered the couches so there was no sitting comfortably unless you first wanted to fold and put away that laundry. Piles of junk mail and papers were stacked on the coffee and end tables alongside overly dusty knickknacks. The kitchen and bathrooms always needed more attention than was ever given.

Dogs would come in and out of the trailer, so dog hair stuck to everything fabric, including our clothing. The trailer still didn't come close to the filth I'd grown up in with Sarah though. I always had chores to do at Brenda's house, but at least I never had to pull dried dog shit out of the carpet.

Brenda didn't care for me much, and I don't blame her at all. I had a terrible attitude and a terrible temper, and it didn't help that Robert constantly compared me to her own children, which really upset her. Understandably. I wonder how it made her feel when Robert would kiss me on the lips? I wonder if she ever thought that it was odd that Robert would kiss his own "daughter" that way. She never asked me how I felt about it, but for me, it was so extremely unsettling. Every single time, I felt sick to my stomach, especially as he'd already tried to molest me in the past, and we both knew it. Since I never said anything though, he'd kiss my lips right in front of his wife.

I also never said anything about the time I traveled with them to Colorado on vacation. We went to see Robert's family there. The town was so pretty and smelled so pretty too. It was like a movie set of a small mountain town. Robert's elderly parents lived in a tiny little trailer in a tiny little trailer court with a tiny little patch of well-manicured grass in the front. That didn't allow them room for a lot of company all at once, so some of us slept on the floor of the living area. That was fine with me as I'd slept in rougher places. It took only one night to realize that Robert and the person he called Dad were the same type of person.

As I lay sleeping on that trailer floor, I was awakened by my "grandpa" down by my feet, putting his hands up my pajama bottoms, under my panties, and touching my vagina. I instantly woke right up and looked him in the face. Getting up fast, I made my way past the other kids on the floor and went into the bathroom. I'm sure I scared him. Why the fuck did he do that? Why did he think I wasn't going to wake up? Did any of the other kids see what had happened?

When I had the courage to come out, he was gone of course, and it appeared that everyone else was still asleep. I've always wondered if anyone else was awake that night. I won't ever get to confront him, of course, because that old man is far dead by now thanks to a lifestyle of shitty eating habits. Robert is dead too. I pretended to care and be sad at his death, because that was what was expected of me. I was known to be Robert's only daughter, but the truth is that he really does have a biological daughter out there somewhere. I overheard a conversation when I was little about Robert molesting that girl child. As I've mentioned, in the eighties and nineties, nobody around me gave a shit about the heart, mind, or body of a child. I didn't give a damn that Robert died, and it would have done zero good to tell Sarah about Robert when he was alive. I was a small sacrifice.

We had little money, Mike and I, with which to get out of Robert's place, but Mike did manage to find us a small trailer in a mobile home park in Blue Eye. I hadn't gotten full-time employment yet, so until I did, I babysat kids that lived in the other trailers around us while parents worked. It was okay. I made enough money each week to keep Mike off my ass about helping to provide. Every dollar I made went directly into Mike's pockets. He made sure to remind me frequently that, if wasn't for him and his mom, David and I would have been homeless in Bartlesville, so he'd ultimately saved us. We lived in his house and ate his food, and he had taken care of us back then when I needed it—even though we were a couple and I'd immediately taken on total responsibility for Mike Jr. with regards to his care and wellbeing. As such, it was only fair that I give Mike all of my earnings now. Okay, Mike.

While I kept kids to make money, Mike spent his time in Branson. He was always looking for opportunities to make money, legal or not. Eventually, Mike opened an auto-mechanic business in Branson: Walkers Auto and RV. He was very good at his job. I know I tell you all of these negative things about Mike, but I have to say that he got things done. His customers loved him. To them, he was great! Mike had a brilliant business mind, and he was also a very talented mechanic. The rumor was that there wasn't anything with a motor that Mike couldn't fix, and that was the truest rumor ever. On his business cards, he promised he could fix trucks, cars, boats, and RVs, which he did. When word got around about Mike and his shop, his business was soon booming. People brought their stuff from all over the place because they knew Mike would fix the problem. He could charge people what he wanted, and they would pay him.

Aside from Mike's guaranteed quality work, people saw in him a hard-working father with a family full of boys and his little wifey by his side. People loved Mike's charm. The guy had so much charisma he could talk to any guy about any subject and make any female of any age blush with his giggle. Mike sure had a way with people. He loved attention. So many people publicly and privately knew of Mike somehow. Everyone knew his name.

A couple of times Mike fixed cars for free. They usually belonged to single moms with no money. You're wrong if you think that didn't get him praise. Yes, that was great what he did but know that it wasn't out of the kindness of his heart but rather for the recognition. Of course, it worked. Everyone loved this guy. Everyone except for me.

I hadn't been watching kids long before I also got a job as a housekeeper at a resort in Branson. Time shares and condos are a huge thing there because of the year-round tourism. That place doesn't stop making money. It was harder for me to get work at first, mainly because I had a toddler at home for whom I couldn't afford daycare, and with Mike insisting that I stay home, it was okay for a while. I didn't want to stay home anymore though. Mike was gone all day, all the boys were in school now, so if I didn't have any kids to watch, for whatever reason, I didn't make money. I wanted a job, and I wanted to meet other people. I was starving for friendship or at least something that wasn't full of Mike.

It was 2003 when I finally got to go out into Branson and work. A family had moved in across the way who had a teen-aged daughter. Mike had talked to her parents about helping with the boys while he and I worked. It worked out fine for a while. I cleaned condominiums for a timeshare resort, so there was always work for a first and second shift. I started out with a rotating schedule and worked my fair share of second shifts, while Cindi, our new teen babysitter, helped me with the house chores and the three boys. She was very good at it. If it was a second-shift day, Cindi would come right in from school to tend to my kids just as I would be on my way out the door to work. When I returned in the late afternoon, Cindi always had my kids tucked into bed and the trailer cleaned up. Sometimes she would be asleep on the couch, and other times she would be gone, and Mike would be asleep in our room.

At first, I was happy to have Cindi there helping out. She did take some stuff off my plate as far as the kids and chores were concerned. More importantly, Mike was always in a much better mood when Cindi was around. Not only did she help me around the house, but she was helpful to him as well. In 2003, Mike and I both were turning twenty-three. Cindi was fourteen when we met her, though she didn't look like a regular fourteen-year-old. She was well over five feet tall, had very long blonde hair and very icy-blue eyes that she kept extenuated with dark eye makeup, and her body should have belonged to a fully adult woman and not a child. She was proud of her body, and she made it obvious that she was. She wore clothing that showed every curve of her not-so-childlike body, and it very much attracted people's attention—Mike's in particular.

Pretty soon, my partner and the father of my second child soon began to point out differences between Cindi and myself. He constantly made references to Cindi looking like a California girl, pointing out that she would be the type of girl to which he was normally attracted. He told me how beautiful and blue Cindi's eyes were, while mine were just brown. He talked of how pretty her hair was, long and blonde, while mine was just brown.

He pointed out how Cindi was so fashionable and me . . . not so much.

What he really did was help me to understand that he and my teen babysitter/neighbor were sleeping together. Of course, they were. Cindi literally became Mike's best friend. No matter what shift I worked, or where I was even, Mike and Cindi were together. All the time. I'd come home from work to find the two of them just hanging out as happy as can be. He was always happier when Cindi was there. If I wasn't at work and was home with the kids, Mike and Cindi were together still. She was with Mike everywhere he went. I grew to hate Cindi quickly.

Yes, Mike had a lighter mood when Cindi was there, but he criticized and made fun of me more. He played and laughed with Cindi right in front of me, and she played and laughed right along with him. Those fucks had a huge crush on each other and didn't do anything to hide it. They didn't care that I was right there in the same room, and Mike didn't care that Cindi wasn't eighteen. No matter how Cindi felt about it, what Mike was doing was rape. Of course, when I brought it up with Mike, he'd say that it wasn't happening and that I was imagining things. Mike told me I was paranoid and that I needed to stop being so mean to Cindi. He said that it wasn't Cindi's fault that I was so ghetto and had low self-esteem, and he defended her right to hang out in our house. "Cindi helps so much! You should be happy to have her here."

Cindi's parents didn't think it was rape either. They loved Mike being around as much as Cindi did. After all, they weren't going to be mad at the guy who kept them supplied with weed. They could also see with their own eyes how good Mike treated Cindi, and that I was just crazy, really. I'm sure they wondered, *How does Mike put up with her? He is so nice to Cindi and keeps the pot supply coming. Mike must be a good guy*. It didn't matter to them one bit that an adult man with a partner and kids was pursuing their teen daughter or that they had a sexual relationship. Nobody saw a problem with that. Way to protect. No police report would be made there.

Other people in the trailer court saw it too. They didn't try to hide their relationship from anyone. They didn't have to. Nobody was going to say shit about what Mike was doing. Why? Because Mike had too much to offer people. He was the auto-mechanic, the cool guy on the block who was willing to offer help when help was needed. Mainly though, it was because Mike was the weed guy, and nobody gave enough of a shit about me to say anything against him. He even had people lying for him. I could see Mike and Cindi right in front of my face, but if I tried to confide in any of those people, every damn person would defend Mike and act oblivious. How could they not know? Any time Mike left to go anyplace, Cindi was right in the car with him, and I was at home with my children.

This went on for such a long time that I started to feel like I was losing my mind. I knew exactly what was happening, but he had everyone so convinced that he was good. I also knew that Mike loved Cindi, and she loved him. It was so obvious every time they opened their mouths to speak to each other. She made Mike laugh in a way that he never laughed with me. Just the expression on his face, the way Mike looked at Cindi, broke my heart. They openly loved each other, and I only existed to take care of the children. What had happened?!

There was absolutely no way to plead my case. Anytime I opened my mouth about Cindi and tried to confront him about their affair, he bashed me and told me how shitty I was and again how I was paranoid and needed mental help. He'd also suggest that, if I did something to make myself prettier, then I wouldn't be so worried about Cindi. "Your low self-esteem isn't Cindi's fault, Lu." No, I suppose it wasn't, but I still wished she would just go away. Cindi didn't go away, but we did end up moving out of that trailer park. I am pretty sure we got evicted. Mike and our landlord didn't get along too well. Maybe our landlord was the one person who could see through Mike's bullshit.

No matter whether or not Cindi was a willing party to what Mike was doing, it was wrong. It was rape. I wish I would have had the courage to go to the police. If I would have, Mike would have been arrested and sent to jail. All I would have had to do is give them my bedsheets. Mike had more sex with Cindi on those sheets than he had with me. Mike would have been gone, and me and the kids would have been free. Of course, if that was how it had happened, Mike wouldn't have been around long enough to give me my own beautiful little girl later. I should be more apologetic for not protecting Cindi from Mike, but it's hard with her, that double-edged sword I have for her.

After we left the trailer park, we moved around some before settling into a house at the end of a cul-de-sac in Hollister, Missouri. It was a nice little home with three bedrooms, two bathrooms, a nice fenced-in backyard, sliding glass doors in the back, and pretty kitchen countertops. Even though it was a cookie-cutter house, it was still the nicest place I had ever lived.

At one point while we were there, my brother Ralph came to stay with us for a short while before finding out that he might become a father and went back home. My sister, Sandra, also came to stay with us, but her visit was short-lived as well. Although Ralph had external reasons for leaving, the real reason neither of them stayed long was the relentless fighting between me and Mike.

It also didn't help that Cindi was still in the picture. I told you that Cindi and Mike were best friends, and there wasn't anything I could have done about it aside from calling the police to stop it. Mike loved Cindi, and he wasn't afraid to be physical with me if I mentioned the word "police." I could only try to defend myself so long, mentally and physically, before I got tired. And I did. I got tired of trying to convince Mike to love me the same way he loved Cindi. So, I gave in. I just gave up and let it happen. I thought that, if I did, then Mike would love me too. He didn't though, and I only made things worse for myself.

I stopped fighting with Mike and Cindi. He was never going to make her go away. They were like devils to my soul, and I wanted peace. I wanted happiness. That's all I had ever wanted: just to be happy. I wanted to be wanted. I wanted to be a normal, happy, regular person, but it was already too late for all of those things.

Mike saw that I was giving in. He saw that I was breaking, and he took full advantage. I gave in so much that I thought I wanted to be more like Cindi. I hated my brown skin, I hated my brown hair, and I hated looking into my own brown eyes. Why did I have to be so ugly? When I was a kid, James, Mel, and Johnnie used to tell me how beautiful I was while I was being molested, and now as an adult, I was ugly, ghetto, and not good enough? It didn't seem fair. I tried several times to turn my brown hair blonde, but each attempt left my hair orange and me even less pretty. For a moment, I liked Cindi more than I liked myself. Cindi made Mike happy, and I didn't. I fully hated myself.

Mike saw that I was broken and preyed on my brokenness. He started to feed me Xanax. That played its part, helping me to escape from some of the emotional pain constantly seeping out of me. I was a slave to Mike, physically, mentally, and emotionally. I tried everything to convince Mike to love me the same way he had before—or the way I thought he had at least. I knew that Mike would never love me, but at that point, I still hoped that he would. I needed him to. I was falling apart, and I needed Mike. I needed my companion . . . the one who should have been there for me but instead was doing his part to slowly chip away at me.

I completely submitted. I took full care of the children, did every ounce of housework, cooked every meal, did all the laundry, worked a full-time job, and handed over all of my earnings to Mike. (Because he had saved me from being homeless. Remember?) I did these things for my family while Mike and Cindi spent time together on my bed, in the room I shared with him. They were always carrying on. By that time, Mike was so bold that he had even begun to call Cindi his girlfriend right in front of me. It made no difference to me. I didn't give a fuck about it at that point. As long as she was keeping him happy in the bedroom, then he wasn't out in the rest of the house, getting in my face.

I've told you that I was responsible for preparing all the meals. If Cindi was there, then I would have to prep plates for two and deliver them to my room, because they didn't eat dinner with the rest of us. I'd serve the children, clean up, and turn off the kitchen lights, but not before retrieving the dishes from Mike and Cindi. There was no need for Cindi to help with anything. She'd gone from being my helper, with the kids and chores, to being Mike's best friend and fuck pal. She'd turned into just another person I had to wait on. Like I said though, Mike was feeding me Xanax to keep me mellow, and eventually, I became emotionless.

By 2005, Mike Walker had been draining the life out of me, in every way he could, for five years. On my birthday, we went to the lake "as a family," which of course included Cindi. I spent that birthday drinking beers alone and tending to my kids, while Mike and Cindi played games both behind my back and in front of me. *Fuck Lu!* they thought. I was depressed enough, it was dark enough, and I was busy enough chasing kids that they were sure I wouldn't mind them playing around in the deep water together. They did it and didn't care about what was happening to me.

And in the end, they did fuck me. I so desperately wanted what Mike had with Cindi that I allowed Mike to pull me into a threesome with the two of them. It didn't matter to me what had to happen. Mike was supposed to be mine. He had wanted me in the beginning, and then he'd stopped. We had our boys together. I just wanted his attention. I let him convince me that it was okay, and that it would make us a stronger family. It didn't do that at all.

Cindi was about to turn eighteen now, and her parents just didn't care anymore that she basically lived at my house, so threesomes fueled by weed and Xanax became a regular thing. But if you can fucking imagine, Cindi began to get crazy jealous and showed it plainly. She hated the fact that Mike was being somewhat nicer to me. He actually was a little. It was fake, of course, but at the time it seemed like he was being just a little softer to me. Damn Cindi hated that, and she wasn't going to have it. Very soon, Cindi grew very open about the fact that she wanted Mike all to herself, without me in the picture. And whatever Cindi wanted, Cindi got.

I started getting locked out of my own bedroom with Mike and Cindi on the other side of the door doing whatever they pleased. It made me crazy. I cried so much. Every time, my boys had to watch me yell and beg for Mike to let me in. *"Open the fucking door!"* I don't know how I did not die on the outside of that bedroom door, pleading for Mike—pleading for the person who was supposed to love me. Eventually I came to a breaking point when I woke up to the two of them having sex right next to me in the same bed. We always slept in the same bed. I had no control over that. As you sit here and judge me, know that I had no control over anything. I was completely under the control of a narcissist. I don't know how many times they pulled it off without me knowing, but that was the first time they woke me up with full on sex happening next to me.

When I asked them to stop, Mike said the same thing to me: stop. He just kept doing what he was doing, told me to stop complaining, and pointed out that I had him all to myself when Cindi wasn't there. But she was always there. After realizing that

I couldn't interrupt them at all, I got up out of bed, took my cigarettes, and locked myself in the closet, not coming out until morning. I cried so much that night. I cried more that night than I ever did as child, no matter what form of abuse I was suffering through.As a child, I'd become numb to feelings. I learned how to put things in my box of memories and not think about my daily life of sexual assault or physical abuse. I cried more that night than Shannon could ever make me cry punching me with his fists. Shannon was loud obnoxious and just an all-around loser, but Mike was different.

Chapter 10

I got to the point where even the sound of Mike's voice caused me incredible anxiety. The sound of his voice caused me fear. One day in 2005, I finally lost it. I was in the kitchen of that cul-de-sac house, and I snapped.

Mike is so cold-hearted. He knew how to withdraw affection and be distant. That was one of the ways he'd get to me on purpose. He would just stop talking to me. If he was in any kind of mood, which he always was (because he's the fucking devil), then he could just completely turn away from me. No words, no emotions, no eye contact, no nothing. That was normally the way he behaved if Cindi had to leave for some reason; he just walked around, ignoring me, and texting back and forth on his phone. I always knew who he was texting.

That would make me beg for his attention even more. The louder I was and the more I cried and begged for him, the more he pushed me away. "You're a crazy Indian, Lu! That's what's wrong with you!"

That day in 2005 turned into one of those days. I begged and begged for Mike to hold me. I needed to be hugged. I felt so out of control, and I needed help. Instead, Mike acted like he was scared to death to be around me and completely left me alone, looking at me from across the room with an expression that declared he was clueless as to why I would be so wound up. Like he was oblivious as to why I was hurting so much inside.

I picked up a kitchen knife and literally began hacking down at my arm. There were no slicing motions, just me hacking down at my arm like it was fucking tree limb. That was so stupid. I'm thankful that the knife wasn't sharp, and I didn't seriously wound myself, though I did go to the hospital. The wounds were only superficial but guess what? Mike was more than willing to talk to them about how I'd had a mental breakdown and 'tried to kill myself.' That loss of control landed me under a seventy-two-hour suicide watch at a facility in Springfield, Missouri. It wasn't me who deserved to be there, but it was me who had to go.

My visit consisted of a ton of group counseling, no caffeine after 2:00 p.m., and a lot of other "crazy people" who had their own demons. One Caucasian guy had a very noticeable scab ring all the way around his neck. He had hung himself but was found and cut down before he died. It was intimidating to look at, but I did. I stared at him every time he walked past. I'm sure he never noticed me.

Counseling didn't do a thing for me during those seventy-two hours because I was so full of hate, animosity, and sadness. I didn't know the first thing about how to be truthful with myself let alone other people. What was I to know about opening up to anyone? I couldn't talk to strangers about myself. They didn't need to know me. I didn't need to tell anyone anything. I just wanted to leave, and after seventy-two hours, I did. I went right back home to find long blonde hairs in the bathroom hairbrush. I am Native American remember, and Mike doesn't have long hair. It set me off.

"You're just crazy, Lu."

You have to know that he just threw that shit word around like candy at a parade. He had validation now and was embracing it fully. "You're just crazy, Lu."

We got evicted from that cul-de-sac house, and surprisingly enough, I didn't see Cindi for a while. I mean, I still caught Mike texting, and I'd still wake up to him talking to her on the phone in the middle of the night, but it was a while before I physically saw Cindi with my own eyes. Whatever. That was fine with me. She must've gotten a new boyfriend and was off to ruin someone else's life.

We got a different house in Hollister. Mike still had the automechanic shop, and I was still cleaning condos but for a different set of timeshare properties. I had become good at housekeeping. It seemed to have become my thing, even though sadly I feel that this may have been the beginning of my obsessive-compulsive disorder. Housekeeping has become therapeutic for me. I am full of anxiety and stress, so it's good for me to scrub out my anger.

The job was hard physically, but I didn't mind a bit. Some of my shifts I was able to think about the work, but more often than not, my mind wondered about what Mike was doing and who he was doing it with.

I never felt safe in my thoughts about Mike. I was always paranoid that Mike was out being unfaithful. More often than not, my gut instinct and thought processes were correct. His lies would either reveal themselves or I'd catch him in them. When I did catch him, he just pounded that paranoia right back into me instead of just admitting anything. The guy had more girlfriends than I'm sure I knew about. I wasn't good enough for Mike. Ever.

There were a couple of times that I did push back and found the courage to leave, but each time I did, Mike would guilt me into coming right back. He'd tell me that it would be impossible for me to raise our kids alone. He said that I would never be financially stable enough to support them alone. He said that the kids would hate me for taking them away from their father, and because of that, I would never have a good relationship with my children. He even tried to tell me that my sons would turn out gay if raised by a woman. Once more, okay Mike. Every time though, it worked. Every time, he was able to convince me that I couldn't do it alone, and I'd return to the exact same thing that had caused me to leave: Mike's cold and brutal nature. A million times over, Mike had proven that he didn't give a shit about my feelings.

One of those times that Mike couldn't have cared less was one of the times I left with my kids but ended up right back home. When I got back that specific time, I came back to find Crickett living in the house. Yes, you did read that correctly. I couldn't have been gone more than a week or so. Every time I left Mike, my brother Ralph took us in. There was never a time that Ralph wasn't there for me.

This time, when I had returned to Mike with the kids, Crickett had made her way from California to Missouri so that she could live in the house with us. This same house I had been trying to get away from without ever finding the courage to stay gone. I'm extremely positive this just didn't happen on a whim. Mike had always wanted two women in the house. As much as he hated women, he wanted to control them. Mike blames every woman for ruining his life. His mother Cindy for leaving him as a baby, Dina for pushing him to the side, and Crickett for lying to him about birth control. I had been ruining Mike's life for almost six years by the time Crickett came back into the picture. Still, he needed to feel like a fucking king by having two women in his house. He needed his power validated by having the two of us there to control. I knew what Mike was aiming for, and that sure as fuck wasn't going to happen.

Much like with my situation with Cindi, Mike's little fucking tart in Missouri, there wasn't anything I could do or say to make

Crickett leave. Mike had let her in. I had to accept the fact that she was there. No number of tears on my part would convince Mike that this arrangement wasn't okay. Mike Jr. had his real mom back though. I'm sure the poor little guy had to have been sick of women coming and going by that point. Crickett was back. His mother, who had left him not once but twice for California. His mother, who hadn't cuddled her sick or sad little boy in more than five years because she was half a country away. She was here now and allegedly to stay. How could she be a mom now? Nonetheless, she was here.

As far as Mike was concerned, it was great that Crickett was back, because he needed someone at the office to answer the phone and do bookkeeping. Yeah, I know, how come I couldn't do that for Mike? I could have helped and been part of the family business, but Mike said I was absolutely helping the family business by letting him work as much as he needed, and I did my part by taking care of the kids. Mainly though, he kept me at home because how else could he possibly have Cindi or Crickett (or whatever other girl he had at the time) there with him to validate not only his achievements but his own greatness. I couldn't be in the office to interrupt that. I had to be secure at home in a position where it wasn't possible for me to leave.

Crickett's ass wasn't telling any of Mike's secrets either. She was very secure in her position. Besides, she had no loyalty to me at all. What did she owe me besides maybe a "thank you" for raising her son? You know, for hating Crickett as much as he did, Mike sure was happy to have her around. It's like he had a new best friend all over again. I listened to the two of them laugh and carry on about the people, places, and things from their old life together in California—memories of a past that I knew nothing of, so I had nothing to offer. It was annoying, and it hurt to see them laughing together. What was I going to do besides nothing?

With me being the obvious maid to the family, I was always washing, folding, and putting away laundry. Not just mine and the kids' but everyone's. Crickett technically washed her own laundry, but if it was left in the washer or dryer when she used the machines, it was very much expected that I finish her laundry process, from drying to folding to delivering it to her room. One day while taking care of Crickett's responsibility, I found a pair of my own panties in her wash. Of course, Mike said that it was an obvious mistake, and that our dirty laundry must've just been mixed up, that I needed to stop being so rude and disrespectful to Crickett for my own mistake, and that I better let up on her because she's "here to help run the family business, Lu."

Then there were the times I woke in the night to find myself alone in the house with the children. Where were Mike and Crickett? I knew exactly where they were, of course. I'd lock the kids in the house and drive to the shop where I'd find the two of them high on meth yet still having the nerve to question me as to why I was out of the house.

The shop was Mike's safe zone. Him, his co-worker (before he too got sick of Mike and left), Crickett, and whichever other low life they had hanging with them at the time could always be found somewhere around that shop. I'm sure that's why the police started watching it . . . and watching our house as well.

Chapter 11

Mike thought he was on top of the world. He could do whatever he wanted without consequence. His shop was making money, and his reputation for reliable work was widespread. He'd done so much work in the Branson area that other business owners would give Mike little perks. Those little perks did a lot to swell Mike's ego.

Before the kind of a person Mike really was came to light, he was also able to do some jobs for local law enforcement. That gave him something more to brag about. "They love me, Lu." Well, while Mike had his nice-guy persona and great reputation among the business community, he also had a low-key rep with a different crowd for selling pounds of weed out of our house. That's something most townspeople didn't know about Mike until it came out in the newspaper.

Because Mike is such a good-looking guy, despite his Jekyll/Hyde personality, he had girlfriends. His business ownership required people to need him at all hours of the night, so he didn't have a specific time that was reasonable for him to be home. As such, he got home whenever he pleased. "I'm a business owner,

Lu. Clients need me." These clients included women who waited for him at the bar.

Mike didn't drink or smoke, but he sure did enjoy being a bar fly. He liked to hang around, play pool, and socialize. By "socialize" I mean giggle around with the women who were gaga over him. It was ridiculous. Some of those people would be willing to die keeping Mike's secrets and others couldn't wait to send me texts about who was sitting on Mike's lap.

Mike didn't need to drink to have a good time. By nature, Mike *was* the party. He also didn't need to drink to be a monster. The evil he spewed came naturally from his soul. Mike says he hated women who smoked cigarettes—especially if it was me who was the smoker, which he refused to allow—which is another reason I didn't understand his need for bar women. He hated all women smokers except, of course, when it came to his little best friend Cindi. She could do whatever she pleased, and he worshipped the ground she walked on. He'd even bought Cindi's cigarettes because (remember) she wasn't eighteen.

If Mike saw me with a cigarette, he'd literally try to break my fingers to get it away, always grabbing my hand with his and squeezing to the point of pain while scolding me, telling me how ugly I looked and how I tasted like an ashtray. Oh, I still smoked though. I needed those cigarettes then just like I had when I was a kid. It was my only escape. Fuck Mike. I just had to do it when he wasn't around. He had me in panic mode every second of the day.

I started smoking wooden-tipped "Black and Mild" cigars by the pack. I'm sure that those contributed to my asthma. I'd hurry and smoke them down while he was gone, then have my teeth brushed and face washed by the time he returned. When we were in an open, crazy fight though, I'd just smoke right in front of him and accept the consequences. Fuck it.

Mike had all kinds of buddies—his "amigos" is what he called them. Mike was moving drugs by the pound, so of course, he had all types of buddies of all ages. Old and young, rich and poor, completely normal and all types of strange. Mike knew people. But not everyone who Mike thought was his "amigo" really was.

The first time our house was raided by COMET (Combined Ozarks Multi-Jurisdictional Enforcement Team), I was just three or four months pregnant with my only daughter. It was well into the night because everyone in the house was asleep. The search warrant specified "11:00 p.m."

BOOM!!!!

I heard what sounded like an explosion and then loud voices. Then I saw flashes of light and felt hands grabbing my pregnant body and dragging me from the bed. Then I was being handcuffed. I looked over and the same thing was happening to Mike. We were taken out of the master bedroom and through the dining area. That's when I saw the back door, or more specifically, the lack of a back door. What was left was completely busted to pieces and what was left was hanging open. Mike and I were walked through the dining area and into the living room, where all three of my sons, the oldest no more than nine, were also handcuffed and sitting against the wall. Along with them was Mike's younger brother, Bubba, who was from California but living with us and working for Mike at the shop. I sat against the wall, scared for myself and my sons as we watched the police tear our entire home apart.

Every inch of our house was ransacked. Every room was ripped apart. They pulled out cabinets and drawers, emptying all contents onto the floors. They pulled everything from all of our closets, turned over beds, and emptied out toy boxes. Nothing was spared from being dumped out or ripped open. They were looking for the pounds of weed Mike was selling. I'll say right damn now that I was a pot smoker, not a drug dealer. Mike didn't allow me to know one single thing about shit. I wasn't allowed in the room when people came over. I was to mind my own business and nothing more. I didn't ask questions, nor was I allowed to. Mike says he did that for a reason: If I didn't know anything, then I couldn't tell on him. Mike didn't have to keep me in the dark to keep me quiet. I was scared to death of Mike. I wasn't saying a word. It's not like I didn't have a good idea of what was happening, but I played stupid like I was supposed to.

They tore apart every inch of our home, turned our world upside down, and found nothing. Apparently, nobody had done enough research to know that Mike didn't nickel and dime anything. He only let go of large quantities at a time, so that made it less likely that he'd have product in the house for extended periods of time. Also, Mike had the shop.

We got uncuffed, and Mike was taken into custody for twenty-four hours. I didn't get arrested because that shit wasn't about me. Thankfully, I was just the family servant who did as I was told and wasn't allowed a voice. It sucked for Mike though, because we lived in a large community—a community in which he'd gone out of his way to be known (in one way or another). With this raid by the drug taskforce, his name ended up on the front page, which started to make things a little tough for Mike. His reputation had been majorly tarnished.

Do you honestly think that Mike gave a fuck about that paper though? He didn't. But he also lost his good standing with his bank. I say "his" bank because I wasn't allowed to have any kind of account. Every dollar earned went directly to him. He lost good standing with other business owners as well, and eventually, business slowed at the shop. None of this stopped him. So stubborn, immoral, and selfish, Mike thought that he was above the law, and above everyone else. *"I'm Mike Dog, Lu!"* Oh, and speaking of the law, he obviously wasn't working on law-enforcement vehicles any longer, and instead, his "buddies" began to watch his shop.

Crickett, Mike Jr.'s "real mom," was still around at this point. She'd hooked up with Mike's younger brother, Bubba. Fucking weird-ass people. But guess who was super cool with the situation? Mike. He wanted Crickett to stay around and found it comforting that she was with his younger brother, which he figured also helped solidify his secrets. Nobody but me thought that was odd, probably because literally everyone but me was smoking meth. I'm not saying that as a joke. Mike, Bubba, Crickett, the shop employee . . . everyone was running around high on meth and not concerned with already having been raided once by COMET. That stupid, stupid asshole Mike was even still selling bricks of marijuana out of our house.

The only reason we didn't get evicted the first time we were raided was that Mike was such a master manipulator that he convinced them to let us stay. Or maybe it had to do with money. To be honest, I don't know how we got to stay in that rental house after the police tore it apart because of what was happening inside. Mike had also rented the little, tiny house right next door—like *literally* next door, fifteen steps away, and then moved his younger brother Bubba and Crickett into it.

Since Mike Jr. was a young boy, I don't suppose anyone thought to ask him how he felt about his mother leaving, coming back, at one point carrying on a couple of lesbian relationships (a whole other story I'm not getting into), and now being in a relationship with his biological uncle . . . all while his little eyes were watching. He watched this relationship between his mother and his uncle, and his own father cheering it on from the sidelines to benefit his own financial gain. For a stepmom, he had an emotional wreck of a human being who was just trying to hold herself together instead of splitting apart at the seams. And all for the sake of what? The poor guy was stuck in an adult tornado.

All of the boys were. A toxic adult tornado. I know that Mike Jr. had to have felt my anxiety and anger.

I know that he didn't have a good mom in me, because I was mad at him. I was mad at him for what his parents were doing, and it absolutely wasn't anywhere near his fault. None of their toxic behavior had anything to do with him. All he needed was a good raising. He hadn't asked for any of this. Was he a hard boy for me to raise for ten years? Yes, he was, but (again) it was not his fault. He was born from a toxic relationship that more than likely was built on a foundation of drugs, lust, and lies. His own mother left him as a toddler to be raised by a father who was a psychopath and a stepmom who was already emotionally damaged before even meeting him. I took things out on Mike Jr. that weren't his doing. I didn't love him the way that I should have, and he felt it.

I wish that I could have been a different person for you, Mike Jr. You needed and deserved a mother to love you like you were her own. Because of my hatred and animosity towards Mike, I failed at being a mother for you. You always deserved love, care, and nurturing. You deserved a real mom. I was so angry because I didn't even know how to be a good mother to my own baby yet, when I suddenly had another little boy who was pissed at me as soon as I came into his life because of his own damn parents. Mike Jr., I am so sorry, and I only wish that someday you can forgive me for not giving you more of myself as a mom. I swear, in front of God, that I was just struggling to know my place.

My daughter, Lily, was probably two weeks old, if that, and I was fresh out of the hospital, when our house got raided again for the second time by the same exact task force that had conducted the first raid. That second raid was a little different, if only because it didn't happen in the middle of the night. I was in the master bathroom and had just stepped out of the shower. I was just wrapped in a towel when I heard yelling coming from the living area. A bunch of yelling. I could hear it but couldn't understand the words. In a panic, I opened the bathroom door in nothing but that towel to find a gun pointed directly at my face. On the other end of that gun was a female SWAT member, telling me that if I moved, I would be shot in the head. My heart sank. At that moment, I only thought about my children. I just knew for sure that they'd be taken from me.

The yelling, of course, was our house being raided again less than a year after the first time. This time they didn't tear things up like they had before. They didn't cuff me or the boys. They only wanted Mike. Bubba was in the living room when the swarm came, and he's the one who had begun the yelling—yelling for Mike—before all hell had broken loose again. I just sat on the floor, holding my kids. Even though Crickett and Bubba lived only footsteps away, they were still at my house at all times of the day. It was 7:00 p.m., and Bubba should have been at his own house, but he wasn't.

After SWAT did their search of the house, Bubba was released, and Mike was taken from our house. Did they find anything this time? Not what they were hoping for, though they didn't come away completely empty-handed, just not enough to press felony charges. From what the snitches—a young couple, maybe in their twenties—had reported to them, Mike was in possession of pounds of weed, and he was—even though they didn't manage to find it that day. That's how little Mike cared about any of us.

Mike could've provided a life for us by himself if he wanted to, without dealing. At the time, he was handsome with a great smile and super-cute dimples that added to the charm he could put on when he wanted. He had a firm, square jawline and strawberry blondish hair that he kept buzzed off because of his high hairline. He was very well built, exceptionally strong, and in my entire life, I'd never met a guy as good with his hands as Mike. Whether his eyes were scary or dreamy depended on who you were, but when he got giggly, he'd hop around and be undeniably cute. Mike was also very smart. He never finished high school, but that didn't stop him from having a good mind for business, and he was great with numbers. *"I'm a numbers guy, Lu."*

At the time, Mike was the smartest guy I knew. It seemed like he could talk to anyone about anything, and he always came out looking as if he knew it all. Mike also knows everything there is to know about mechanics, which had helped his widespread popularity. In the ten years I spent watching Mike, I can't count how many people he impressed with his knowledge of many different topics, and even if he didn't actually know anything about it, he could absolutely fake his way through without an issue because he was also very articulate.

He had so much knowledge to offer, and he could have passed that knowledge on to so many people. If he would have taken a different path in life, then his God-given talents would've been enough to lead him anywhere. If he could have just been more kind-hearted, instead of always harboring ulterior motives for everything he did. If Mike had a heart at all, then things would've been so different. That's not Mike though. He only cares about himself.

Ultimately, anyone who got in his way, or anyone who was even part of "Mike Walker World," was really just a stepping stone, a mat for him to wipe his muddy feet across. If you knew Mike, then you had been used by him in some way—even if you were his children. Mike doesn't really love anyone, which is why he didn't for one minute stop selling weed and meth to whomever he could, even though he didn't need to. Mike had to be "known." He couldn't just sit back and be a normal guy. He wasn't happy if he wasn't involved with something in a big way, and those somethings weren't normally good.

So, we were subjected to another raid. Luckily, they only wanted Mike. I got to stay with my children, and they got to stay with me. I am so thankful to God that Missouri didn't take my children from me. Mike got held a little longer this time but only by a day or so. Crickett and I got a bondsperson and bailed him out. I wish we could've left him there. Not Crickett though. She needed Mike out. She had loyalty to him even after she'd sat back and watched as her little son went through his second drug raid. Why didn't she just take Mike Jr. away from us? I'm sure she probably could have, if she'd just fought hard enough for him. Mike had put us in plenty of positions that could have been considered harmful, right? She didn't though. That's what the combination of meth and Mike can do to a person.

Yes, I do still feel some aggravation towards Crickett about that, but I know that it was Mike. He had the ability to steal a person away from themselves. Instead of her thinking that she should save her son, her focus was on saving Mike. I can't say much though because I was under the same stupid spell. Why did I keep going back once I got away?

The second raid for Mike got him a lot of heat from the police, and his reputation in our large community was completely ruined. When COMET had raided the second time, they'd also raided the shop, hoping to find a jackpot in one place or the other. They didn't. All they found was some paraphernalia and personal-use marijuana that couldn't lead to a felony charge. What the taskforce was looking for, and what they'd be so angry to know, was that everything they wanted was about fifteen steps away inside the little house next door.

Mike proudly boasted later about the four pounds they didn't find. Somehow, COMET had failed to bring a drug-sniffing dog both times they raided. That's just crazy. The reason Mike had Bubba and Crickett living right next door was so that he'd have yet another stash spot. In the driveway of the little house next door was a work truck with a visible advertisement on the side: Walkers Auto and RV services. They police never once bothered to look that way. I don't understand to this day how they missed that.

That's the kind of shit that fed Mike's ego. He had confidence that he was smarter than the authorities when it was just dumb fucking luck. When I look back, it's strange to me how many times Mike should have been in trouble but was somehow able to weasel his way out, which grew his ego and persona every time it happened.

Like I said though, this second raid pretty much ruined Mike in Missouri. He couldn't turn a corner without the police looking at him. He had lost all his business and had to shut down the shop. Nobody was willing to do business with him outside of the shop either. Mike was hot. He'd lost his standing in the community completely. He was an enemy now, and that hurt him more than anything. Mike didn't care about police, jail, consequences, or any authority at all. Mike did exactly what he wanted and when he wanted. But with his reputation completely flushed, he was at an all-time low.

That's what affected him the most. Not his children, not me, not our life together, nothing. But if he thought people didn't like him, he was crushed. He wanted to be known. He wanted to be "the guy." His narcissism shone so brightly that when people turned away from him, it ate him from the inside out.

And who do you think was the one absorbing all Mike's anger about this? Who do you think was there to endure all of his rage when he felt like his world was done? Not Cindi or Crickett. It was me. Lu. Of course, this was all my fault! If I had never led him to Missouri, then none of this would have happened to him.

Fuck you, Mike.

Chapter 12

The day that the kids and I left Missouri for Oklahoma, it was exactly that: just me and the kids. By 2009, Mike had single-handedly ruined our lives in Missouri, to the point where we needed to leave the state. Obviously, we didn't get to remain after the second raid on the house. I can only imagine how angry the owners were to have their house ruined. Twice. As a matter of fact, I never got to meet the owners. Mike handled everything when it came to them. Every person Mike had encountered in Missouri was done with him. My kids and I were just part of his wreckage.

My children and I loaded up our Dodge Coronet and got on the road back to Bartlesville, Oklahoma. I had twenty-four dollars cash, a full tank of gas, a car full of our belongings, and four children relying on me for safety. I was scared to death.

Mike said that he had to stay behind for a bit because he needed to tie up some loose ends. "Cross all the T's and dot all the I's, you know." More like he needed to hunt down Cindi.

He felt like everything would be perfectly fine. I would be perfectly fine driving that car back to Oklahoma. I begged Mike not to make me take that car because the brakes were bad and the steering column was very loose. Nobody in their right mind would drive that car on the highway, and no man should expect a car full of kids to be safe when doing so, especially an auto-mechanic. Mike knew that I would do it though, and I did. I cried the entire way, with a baby and three sons watching me, but we made it. Those were four of the most horrifying hours of my life.

When the kids and I reached Bartlesville, Cindy (Mike's mom) was waiting for us to arrive. Talk about a negative association, right? Mike's mom shared a name with Mike's teenaged girlfriend—the fucking girl Mike was so gaga over and had flaunted around everywhere—though his mom spelled her name with a "Y" instead of an "I". (Fuck you, Cindi with an "I".) Mike had loved the fact that he already had the name Cindy tattooed on his chest, and when he'd fallen for Cindi, he'd always giggled over it. Stupid. He "just knew" that it was a sign that she was meant to be in his life. Fucking dumb.

I don't remember how long Mike made us wait before he finally met us in Bartlesville. It was a while because I know that we were struggling to buy food. I called him constantly to ask when he would come to be with us. I don't think it was really because I wanted Mike to be there but rather that I knew he was still there doing dirty deeds, and the anxiety of knowing that was killing me. In those years, I was crazy over, about, and now because of Mike. The stress of it all was getting to me.

The house that we were in belonged to Mike's father, Big Sonny. He'd purchased the place in Bartlesville when he'd also moved from California to Oklahoma. Big Sonny was way too much for me. He's too much for any one person to handle. Much like Cindy, Big Sonny was also a meth user. The difference was that Big Sonny was also a meth *cooker*. If you know someone who does that, then you know exactly how hard they are to keep up with.

The first day I met Big Sonny, I began to understand at least some of the reasons why Mike behaved the way he did. Big Sonny was loud, never wrong, and higher than a kite 99 percent of the time. If he was anywhere around, you knew it because of his loud, booming voice. He could be heard from a long way away. Sometimes it was loud laughter, and sometimes loud crazy cussing and arguing, but he was always heard before he was seen. Big Sonny was a huge pain in the ass. That's the only way to really describe him.

Anyways, at some point, Big Sonny had been busted for meth and in jail for a short time, but he had been able to sell his house to Mike for like six dollars (or something ridiculous like that), so the house wouldn't be seized by the police, and selling for so little, it would somehow save Mike tax money. They are so similar, those two. They'd do anything to keep ahold of their material possessions. Neither Mike nor his father cared about people. They only needed their stuff. Their life stories, and my entire life with Mike, made me fully and completely aware that we mattered less than "stuff." Mike would gladly fight over his material possessions before he'd defend me or his children.

While we had been living in Missouri, Big Sonny had gone to prison, and Mike had moved his mom and Billy into that house. At 812 Lupa Street, the house at most was seven hundred square feet, with two tiny bedrooms, one tiny bathroom, one tiny living area, and a kitchen that was the biggest room in the house but infested with cockroaches. *Fuck*. I'd sworn I'd never share a house with roaches again. I immediately started the roach battle in that house, which was unfit to live in. I did everything in my power to keep the roaches from touching my children and their belongings. Mike finally did return to us, and there we stayed—right there in that tiny roach-infested box on Lupa Street.

Cindy had hepatitis C, stemming from a long life of chaos and drug abuse. She also loved to drink vodka. I know that's how she masked the pain from all the hurtful words Mike had screamed at her over the years. One day, Cindy started bleeding and couldn't stop. The doctors told her that it was an internal bleed coming from her stomach. It was an issue that she'd already had one surgery to fix, but Cindy had continued to drink and still did meth. She had eventually bloated so badly that her stomach lining had torn. Her internal organs finally began to shut down, because of her hepatitis C, her rejection of sobriety, and all the related factors of both.

I used to follow her around with a wet bleach rag, wiping up the blood oozing from her, so that my children didn't come in contact with it. She left a blood trail throughout the house. I was sad to see her go through what she did. I felt bad because she loved my kids so much. I knew that she had so many regrets for the way Mike had been raised and that he hadn't been raised by her. She would cry to me, telling stories of sadness, but she could never get Mike to listen to her.

He would always be full of hate for women, blaming them for all things terrible. Except for Cindi. That girl was the only female Mike ever had any concern for. She could never do anything wrong by him. I knew it, and he wasn't afraid to talk about her in front of anyone. It made me hate him so much. I couldn't understand why he had chosen me, since I wasn't ever good enough for him. Why keep me if he didn't want me?

When Mike did come to be with us in the house on Lupa, I was somewhat relieved that he'd actually shown up. I don't know why. It's not like he was happy to see me or to be back with the family. We had inconvenienced him so many times already. Now he was also being inconvenienced by being in a different state than Cindi. Oh yes, we were still fighting over her. Why couldn't I just get past it? Past her? Because he wouldn't let us. He kept her in our conversations. He made sure that she wasn't forgotten. The fucking guy was completely obsessed with that young female.

So, all of us were packed into that little house. Mike was a psychopath. Mike's mother had hep C and would die soon, and Billy was just as confused as I was but still willing to stay and be with her. Poor Billy. He stood no chance against Mike. He couldn't do anything about Mike and his tyranny. Mike made sure Billy understood that he wasn't the man of the house, and in fact, Mike was. He was the alpha male. Poor Billy was just a yo-yo. Cindy would throw him out and call him back. Each time, he'd come right back, just the same as I would. Stupid asshole Mike had inherited that narcissistic trait from both of his parents, and with that, he formed his own kind of evil. He made us all walk on eggshells.

For about nine years by this point, he had cussed me, screamed at me, cheated on me, head-butted me, mentally and emotionally tortured me, and put me in so many positions that made me so afraid for my life and my body that I thought I'd have a heart attack. Mike's attacks became so frequent and so severe that I honestly thought that I would die soon. I just knew that I was going to have a heart attack from the stress, assuming he didn't kill me first. The fights between Mike and I were brutal. We had so many things to fight about, so many things that I had experienced with him since the day we met. Throughout our entire relationship, Mike had been insulting me, taking full advantage of me, and using and abusing me in all senses of the words.

All I really wanted, in the pit of my stomach, was for Mike just to snap out of it, be normal, and love me. To hold only me in his arms, to only think about me, and be with me in passion still. I still wanted a happy, normal family with Mike. But it's hard to have that with someone who hates you. Mike hated me. He told me out loud how much he wished I'd "just kick rocks, Lu!" And I yelled out loud, in desperation, how much I hated what he was doing to us, and that I hated him too. He told me how much he wished I wasn't me, and how he wanted me to be different. He still wished I had blonde hair. He still wished I were prettier. He still wished I weren't so ghetto. He still wished I was more feminine and dressed better. It was constant. Mike made fun of me all of the time like he was a playground bully who'd made me his daily target. And he'd been at it for nine years. Mike told me of all the reasons I made him unhappy and blamed his cheating on those things. According to him, if I would have changed all those things about myself, then it would have "allowed" him to stay faithful. The fact is that it wouldn't have mattered how beautiful I was. Mike would still have been the same person.

By 2009, every sexual encounter I had with Mike was by his choice. I had lost my physical and sexual attraction for him years ago. By that point, Mike's hands made me sick. I shook when Mike came near me. Although I should have known it during our very first time together, hearing him losing it like that on the phone, by 2009 I knew for certain that nothing gentle would ever come from Mike. He had no soft spot in his heart for me, and so I had two options: Give him sex voluntarily or suffer some sort of violence.

It's already been made clear that Mike liked meth, but he didn't need to be high to be brutal to me during sex. Sadistically, that came naturally to him. I was forced to give my body to someone who insulted me on a daily basis. It was always a battle between my heart, my mind, my body, and Mike . . . and he was always the winner. *"Fuck you, Lu."*

I wanted to kill myself. I wanted to vanish off the planet so that my body never had to be touched by his hands or anything else ever again. My body and my flesh were my own, but it didn't really belong to me. Mike was even more sexually sadistic when he was high on meth. When we were on a marijuana high, that didn't affect his body at all, but when he was high from smoking meth, it was completely different. He couldn't get or keep an erection. Well, not with me anyways. When he and Crickett were high together, I don't think he had a problem performing, but I'm sure that was my fault too, for not being "attractive enough."

He used to say things like, "Lu, if you just hung out with me, then it would be fun for the both of us." By this, he would mean that I should smoke meth with him. *That's a huge fuck you, Mike!* I can tell you that, in all our years together, I did that with him less than five times, and every time I did, I hated it and had only done so to make Mike happy. That was one thing that Mike Walker couldn't force me to do regularly though, and I refused to go down that path with him, just like I refused to go down a path of destruction with Sarah, my own mother.

Mike would get high on meth and then insist that I do everything I could, no matter how many hours it took, to give him an orgasm. It made no sense. When Mike did meth, he couldn't possibly get the erection he needed to reach orgasm, but he insisted that I make it happen for him anyway. He would hold the back of my head, forcing me to give him oral sex for what seemed like hours while he remained soft. He'd tell me during this forced act that the reason he couldn't get a hard-on was because of me. That he couldn't get there with me because I was so unattractive, but I still had to keep trying, because it wouldn't be fair to him not to when it was all my fault.

I had to keep going until he was satisfied. He'd make me use my mouth, my hands, and my vagina to satisfy him, knowing the entire time that I couldn't. It wasn't possible because of the chemicals in the drugs. The entire time he would ridicule me for being less than a woman and keep me awake all night and into the morning, fighting with me. He'd say that maybe I was cheating on him and that was the reason I couldn't get emotionally involved enough to get his dick hard.

I used to stay up all night long, defending myself from the psychotic shit he was projecting onto me. That's what shitty people like him do. They feel guilty for something they've done, then they find a victim and unload it all onto them. It didn't feel the least bit sexy that my body was being made to preform sex acts while my ears had to listen to (and my brain had to process) Mike comparing me to someone else. I think that may have been his favorite mind game. I honestly don't know though because he had so many. That one was exceptionally tough though.

Chapter 13

November 23, 2009 wasn't a better day for me than any of the rest, but it was rather more eventful. After leaving Missouri, Mike got meaner. He was feeling the pressure of what he saw as a loss, and he was taking it out on me. We've already established that Mike didn't love me and sure as hell didn't like me. I had become Mike's enemy, and he had plenty to go to war with. Mike saw me as someone he could freely cut down with his words in order to give himself confirmation as the master of our universe. I was the person he could insult and be aggressive with without any feelings of remorse. Mike had become so cold towards me that every waking moment was filled with fear.

November 23, 2009 started out with Mike coming down from popping Xanax, another one of his favorites, and he was just angry. Mike never needed a reason to be angry in order to treat his family like shit. He had never been one for drinking alcohol, and he had only recently started smoking cigarettes to the point where I could say that he actually "smoked," which he never had in all of our years together. Mike liked weed, meth, and Xanax, with meth and Xanax being on completely opposite sides of the drug spectrum. Unfortunately, both of them turned an already narcissistic person into the devil.

That morning, everyone was home: me, Mike, Cindy, Billy, and all four children. Nobody had work or school because it was the Thanksgiving holidays. Mike and I argued every second of the day, which was nothing but normal for us. He was crashing from Xanax, which intensified his meanness. I was mean too, of course, but only because I spent every day in constant fight or flight mode. Being a slave for Mike, and a ragdoll for him to shove around, push from behind, dig his knee into, and press his face against, and taking in all his hateful looks of disdain had by now brought me into a world where there could no longer be any peace.

Mike had the ability to steal the peace away from anyone. As much as I believe that God has soldiers walking on this planet, with that same belief, I know that Satan has his soldiers too, and Mike is very much one of them. If my soul had ever contained feelings of peace, they were buried now, if not stolen completely. By this time with Mike, I can only describe myself as a wild animal that had become crazed by being constantly poked and prodded through the door of its cage. I was going crazy.

That day, Mike was outside in the front yard, standing by the gate, and I was standing in the front doorway at the top of the porch steps. We were arguing, and I said something to Mike as I stepped off the porch. I don't remember my exact words. I'm sure they were hateful and crude, though maybe they weren't. Mike had so much hate for me by that time that I could have said that the grass was green and set him off. Whatever it was that I said, it was enough.

Mike's eyes got huge, round, and red. I might not remember my words, but I'll never forget the look on his face. It was a look that you'd think I would have seen before, but it wasn't. I witnessed the devil looking back at me through Mike's eyes. I say that without sarcasm. I say that with every ounce of truth in my blood. He was still Mike, but in that moment, he was possessed with so much hate . . . I could see it. I felt it deep in my bones.

Then he came after me. Beside me, right off the porch, was the boys' red wagon, so I shoved it at him in hopes of gaining just a second more of time and ran into the house. He came in after me and proceeded to beat my ass in our bedroom. He bounced me off the walls, stopping me from getting away. I protected myself as much as I could from his fists, which were hitting me in the head and on the side of my face. Then I lay on one side as he beat the more vulnerable parts of my body.

Cindy and Billy screamed for him to stop. My four children were crying in the background as they watched what was happening. The house was tiny. There was no privacy. Everyone could see and hear it all happening. For one moment, Mike stopped punching me and turned around to yell at Cindy, his mother, who was standing in her own doorway trying to avoid being physically attacked by Mike herself. I took the opportunity to get up from the futon mattress where I'd fallen.

In my desperate attempt to rid the house of roaches, I'd pulled the floor trims up and lay them away from the walls. Every day, I was dumping roach poison into the floor joints, so the trims stayed untacked. I picked up a piece of that trim, with staples sticking out of it, and I swung it at Mike's head. (It's okay if you laugh, right here. I promise.) I don't know what damage I thought I was about to do with a flimsy piece of floor trim and some staples.

Of course, when Mike tells his side of the story (as he did to the police that day), what I swung at his head was a two by four with nails in it. I wish it had been a damn two by four! That would have been awesome! Sadly, it wasn't.

Mid-swing, I heard Cindy yell, "Duck"! I don't know who she thought she was protecting by yelling that. It was probably just a reflex. She should have just let me hit him, because I don't see that the outcome would have been any different. Mike ducked, and I didn't get to hit him. Instead, Mike threw me out into kitchen with all his might and resumed beating me, with even more anger, accusing me of trying to kill him with "nails to the head." I lay on the busted-up tile floor, my head bouncing off it as he punched me over and over. Again, I could hear my kids screaming and Cindy begging for him to stop. Billy was trying so hard to help me, to pull Mike off me, but it wasn't working. Even though Billy was taller than Mike by several inches, Mike had gone crazy. He wasn't stopping.

Then as I lay on that kitchen floor, in a fetal position, Mike Walker football kicked me in my lower spine as hard as he could. I'd endured beatings my whole life and birthed three children, but I had never felt a pain so intense. When he kicked me, I screamed. I didn't intend to, I wasn't trying to, but the force with which he kicked me just pushed out this agonizing sound. When he struck this final blow to my body, I felt a huge pop, thinking he'd broken me, and heard Cindy scream, "Mike! The police!"

Eventually, Billy managed to help me up from the kitchen floor and into the bedroom I shared with Mike. Before I knew it, the police had Mike cuffed outside, a female sergeant took pictures of my face and body, and then I was carried out on a stretcher to the ambulance waiting outside. Though Mike was arrested, he spent only a few days in jail.

At the hospital, I was X-rayed. Miraculously, there were no breaks or fractures to my back. The hospital staff called Sarah, who at that time lived up in Northwestern Oklahoma, more than two hours away. She eventually showed up and played her stupid little role: "My poor baby! . . . I'm so sorry this happened to you . . . I'm here to take you home . . ." *(Bullshit, bullshit, bullshit)*

Sarah is literally one of the least genuine people I know. Sadly though, I thought I didn't have any other option. *Shit.* I didn't want to go with Sarah of all people. I didn't want to see KD again. I'm sure that I've mentioned that by this point they were back together as man and wife. Talk about having to make choices. *Fuck.*

David, Jacob, my daughter Lily, and I went with her back to Northwestern Oklahoma, from Bartlesville. The kids and I stayed there, with KD, Sarah, and my younger siblings, DJ and Sandra, for just a brief time, less than a week, for two reasons. The first was that the very second Mike got out of jail he was calling, harassing us nonstop. He called Sarah's house. He called their cell phones. He called my cell phone. He didn't have anything to say that I hadn't heard before: The kids would hate me for taking away their father; I didn't have enough money to live on my own; people fight all the time, and they still stay together for the kids, Lu . . . *Blah, blah, blah.*

I can say "blah, blah, blah" now, but that isn't what it felt like in my heart. I can't express how much guilt Mike could lay on a person, especially a vulnerable one. He's a master manipulator. Just days before, he'd beaten me up in front of his mom, Billy, and our four children, and he was still able to make me doubt myself. Why? Haven't you been reading along? My self-esteem was shattered by that point, weathered and eroded until it was nonexistent.

Of course, the second reason was that I hated Sarah and her waste-of-oxygen husband. I couldn't stand to be around them. I couldn't stand the way they looked, lived, smelled, or acted. I couldn't even stand the sound of their voices. I'd already dealt with enough of them insulting me my whole life. In my mind, I had to go back to Bartlesville. I didn't want to. Why in the world would I want to live with someone who made me cry every day? Someone who made me doubt myself as a person every day? Someone who'd recently begun to tell me how much he hated me every day. But how could I possibly live with Sarah and KD? A man and a woman who made me sick to my stomach. Sarah was my own mother. You'd think that having her in my life would be an option I'd feel blessed and happy to have. But of course, that wasn't possible.

I really just couldn't stop thinking about all the words she'd never said to me as a girl: the words of encouragement and love. All the times she hadn't stepped in when KD was taking punishment to a new level. All the times we told her that we were hungry and were left to fend for ourselves. *"There's hot dogs in the fridge."* All the times she ignored our sexual abuse. The time she'd left me with Shannon. The time she asked me if I wanted to have sex with her and my stepdad. And I couldn't stop thinking about all the years I'd needed her as I struggled with Mike without motherly advice.

Every minute I stayed with Sarah, I had flashbacks of all those things. I think it might have been right then that a seed was planted in me, something that would begin to manifest and allow me the courage to cut my bond with her in the future. I couldn't be with Sarah, so I chose to take the kids and go back to Mike instead. I don't know how good I am at making the "right" decisions, but I've definitely had my share of tough ones. At that moment though, I had no choice but to choose.

After everything that had gone down on November 23, there was a protective order filed and a day was set for Mike to appear in court. I had the protective order dropped and back to Mike I went. Nothing was better when I got back, of course.

"Think of the logic, Lu." That's something Mike must have said to me a million times. "Think of the logic, Lu." Anytime I had something to say, he'd shut me down with, "You're not smart, Lu. Think of the logic." Then he would proceed to outsmart and out-talk me until one day I just had nothing left to say. Well, Mike was right about one thing, at that time anyway. I wasn't a logical person. I was a confused person who should have been in mental-health therapy a lifetime ago.

By Christmas of 2009, the kids and I were back in the house on Lupa Street. Cindy was declining fast when we returned. Billy was gone by that time. My kids' grandma was on her deathbed, and Mike was in a state of madness. It's hard to imagine that he could get any worse, but he managed. Little by little, with each passing day, Mike became colder and more sadistic. There was no denying that Mike was the reason that his mother drank herself to death. She had been in and out of the hospital, but nothing else could be done to spare her body. Cindy's organs were actively failing. She knew she was going to die soon and was still desperately seeking Mike's forgiveness. But no. Mike told his mom that she was dying for a reason. He told her that if she would have been a better mother, none of this would be happening to her now. "God is paying you back."

Whether that was true or not, Mike had zero compassion for his dying mother. If that was how Mike really felt in his heart, then why be around her? Why come from California to Oklahoma to be with her in the first place? Mike was nineteen when he decided to "reconcile" with Cindy. In my opinion, Mike had come to Oklahoma to get revenge on Cindy for leaving him as a baby. He'd made his way to Oklahoma and driven her mad. Mission accomplished.

Hospice care came to the house to keep Cindy comfortable until her death. They brought heavy medications to ease the pain of her organs shutting down. It wasn't too long before the nurse caught on to what was happening. Cindy wasn't getting all her meds. Someone else was helping himself to her medications. Just from his behavior, the nurse was smart enough to know who it was. Mike was taking Cindy's meds—the meds that were meant to keep her calm before death. Cindy was taken from the house then and put into a nursing home, where she died in 2010. She passed just weeks before Mike's thirtieth birthday, the year she would have turned fifty.

In Mike's brain, a dying mother meant that he was going to come into a chunk of money. I can't tell you how pissed he was when he found out that it didn't work like that. Cindy had debts, and the debt collectors made sure that her debts to them were paid. By the time Mike got his check, all that was left was about two thousand dollars. He spent it just as I knew he would. Meth people don't care where money comes from. There was no funeral, of course, as Mike decided to have her cremated, which he also had to pay for. Mike planned a day for friends and relatives to meet at the park just down the block from the house to have grilled food and share stories about his mother. My daughter only has one picture of herself and her Grandma Cindy. I tell her how much her grandma loved her and how lucky she was to have had such a gem in her life.

Mike put word out to Billy that he was going to get beaten up, fully blaming Billy for Cindy's rapid decline. Billy had always treated Cindy like a queen, doing everything in the world for her, even though she treated him badly. In every person's life though, they come to a point where, no matter who the ties are with, they must be cut. That's what Billy had done the Thanksgiving before she died. He'd loved her so much, but he knew that she was dying and that he couldn't help her anymore, so he'd left while I was gone. Mike quickly turned on him then, blaming him for leaving when Cindy "needed him the most."

Maybe so, but like I said, nothing in the world was going to save her this time, so I don't blame Billy. I know how much Cindy meant to him. I'm sorry, Billy, that I didn't get to say goodbye to you. I didn't get to say thank you for trying so hard to help me that day in November. I will never forget how good you were to me and my children. They loved you.

So, Cindy was gone, Billy was gone, and now there was no one there to distract Mike from his hatred. He was also overflowing with self-pity. Like I said so many times, Mike treated his mom like trash. He never showed love or compassion for her at all, but when she passed, he needed *so much* sympathy—sympathy that I didn't have to give. I hated his guts by that point. I hated everything right down to the stupid way he stands so arrogantly. I hated the sound of his voice. I hated his presence. As much as I used to beg for Mike, as much as I'd thought I needed him just to be with me, all of that was dead, and I wished that Mike was dead too.

This was about the time I started seeking help for myself. Mike was completely against me having any sort of counseling and told me I was weak. Maybe I was, but I needed someone. I'd begged for Mike, but he wanted nothing to do with anything that might be healing for me. He was trying to wear me down just like he had his own mother.

At this point in time, after I returned to him after the incident on November 23, our household had no real income, and I had yet to begin looking for employment. Mike was making a little money but not the sort that was taxable, and he kept it to himself. This allowed me to apply for assistance from the state of Oklahoma. It was through that assistance program that I found a facility and began my mental-health-therapy journey with Mandi Jordan.

Chapter 14

I can't possibly begin to give you an accurate number of how many times Mike and I were nose to nose, screaming vulgarities at each other at the very top of our lungs. I don't have an accurate count of how many times he had me pinned to the floor with his knee shoved into my inner thigh while his completely ice-cold eyes did their best to intimidate me. I can't tell you how many times I sat alone, holding myself, because I had been destroyed by him that day in one way or another.

I was raw and yet somehow numb at the same time. I think I had been for a long time. That said, over the years, I'd had plenty of heart-stopping moments with Mike. One day, back when I was pregnant in late 2000, he'd made me take a package to the post office for him. I was so scared that I'm surprised the worker didn't notice me trembling. Mike said that nobody would look at me twice because I was pregnant. I guess nobody did. That package contained numerous boxed and bagged food items, along with a small white brick. Mike always had something about him that allowed him to escape punishment for his actions, and so he was able to be unconcerned. I (on the other hand) was truly frightened.

I honestly don't have it in me to explain every time Mike tortured my soul, my very being, by trapping me there with the children and making me keep it together while I was completely falling apart. Those nights when I knew Mike was out partying while I sat at home full of tears, snot, and anxiety, I still had to take care of my children. I didn't want them to see me lose it.

Sadly, I did cry so much in front of them. It was impossible for me to hold back the tears. Mike shattered my heart. My self-esteem was at zero. I had nothing left to give the four kids who depended on me. It was so hard to even feed myself because of my anxiety, but I still had to give them food. I had no choice but to battle this wet, heavy blanket of depression while still being a mother. The boys knew though. Kids are smart and can notice bad vibes. My kids didn't need to rely on catching a vibe of course, as they watched firsthand as Mike and I crumbled.

By the end, Mike came and went as he pleased. He had made the decision that he was going to do what he wanted with his life from then on. "I'm having a midlife crisis, Lu . . . I've been working since I was fifteen, and I'm tired, Lu . . . I need some time to myself, Lu . . . It's not my fault, Lu. Crickett knew I didn't want kids until I was twenty-five . . ." Mike told me I could stay in the house and just rent it from him. Mike Jr., of course, would stay with us in the house because (after all) it was Mike Jr.'s property as well. "So, there's no need for me to take him with me, Lu."

Listen, I love Mike Jr., and I'm not trying to be a bitch, but that still doesn't seem very fair. Mike left Mike Jr. at the house with me, even though he hated me and I was a bad mom? Mike's brain wasn't okay. He made no fucking sense. Mike was free to come and go, childless and carefree. I tried to talk to Mike and explain to him that I wasn't in a good place mentally. He refused to listen. He couldn't have cared less about what was wrong with me. Mike never loved me. Not even an ounce. He'd used me for everything he could since day one. He'd drained me. Any ounce of strength or dignity that I may have saved in me from my life before him, he stole from, controlled, and destroyed. In that order.

I begged Mike a lot even though we hated each other, even though I knew every day with Mike was an anxiety attack. I was sure that they were just heart attacks in the making. I didn't care. I begged for him to stay with me still, because I didn't want to be alone with the kids in that state of depression. I felt completely empty. I didn't want to put my feet on the ground. I didn't want to wake up in the morning. I didn't have an ounce of energy in my body, but that didn't matter, because I had no choice but to take care of our four children. No choice at all.

As much as I've said I'd stopped caring, my anxiety was full speed ahead, and all I could think about was Mike being out there and not with us. It sounds ridiculous that Mike could be driving me crazy just by having carefree times out there in the world with no responsibilities while I was at the house still giving all of myself to four people.

I wished that I could have had more life experience before becoming a mother. That's how low I'd fallen. I'd look at my kids and think of how much better they'd be without me there, causing them stress. I had nothing to offer. They were all still so young. They needed everything from me, but I was drained and struggling mentally. Mike had split. He'd made it clear that he was backing out. He'd left me. Who was I but someone my young children were watching break down, creating their own bad memories of me? They would be better off without me. I truly believed that.

The very first memory I have is of a man shoving his penis in my mouth. Right from the beginning, from my first years on earth, I'd never been anything to anyone but an object. Other than from Willy B., so many years prior, I am a million percent sure that, at that point in my life, I'd never even had a real hug. I'd never had anyone offer me one and have it truly mean what a hug is supposed to mean. None of that. I certainly never got one from Sarah. I know for damn sure that there was never a day in my life that was ever set aside for just me and her. No mother-daughter bonding. As I got a little older and could understand more, I could feel that she didn't want me, easily picking up her vibes loud and clear. We were her food-stamp dependents. I'd never been anything more to anyone since.

On September 6, 2010, I was going to take things into my own hands. I was sick of memories, sick of abuse, sick of not being able to speak for myself, sick of getting cussed out, sick of knowing that I wasn't meant for anything. *Why am I here?* I was going to finally get away from Mike Walker. I was so certain. Stupid me.

* * *

Liquid charcoal. When I woke up, it was all over my hands and down my front. That's how the nurses were able to get all the Flexeril out of me. Flexeril is a muscle relaxer that I had been taking for a little while. At the time, I'd been in the housekeeping profession nearly ten years, and my body had also been through a lot, so my primary-care doctor had given me Flexeril to help my bunched-up muscles relax and relieve the soreness of constant tension.

That morning, Mike was obviously nowhere around. Who knows where he was? Like I said, he came and went as he pleased. Mike no longer considered me his partner. When he did come into the house, it was only for minutes at a time, and he didn't really speak to me other than to offer some form of criticism, or else he'd be super bubbly, knowing that I was at a low point, and blame me for not being happy. "You see, Lu, this is why I can't be around you." Another head game he had perfected.

That morning, the boys got on the bus for school. When I knew that they had gone, I took care of my daughter and got her ready for the day with breakfast, a bath, and clean clothes. Then I counted out twenty Flexeril and took them all at once. My thought process was that, with Flexeril being a muscle relaxer and my heart being a muscle, if I took enough of them, then my heart would stop. That was my end goal. For my heart to stop beating.

Before when I'd had suicidal thoughts, which was pretty frequent, I'd somehow manage to worry about where my kids would end up. Who would love them as much as I did? Who would die to protect them like I'd always said I would? Who would take care of them until they could be on their own?

I'll tell you that I did have an answer. I only had one person in my entire world that I would trust with my precious little people: my brother Ralph. I knew he could love them the same exact way I did. He had the same childhood fears and knowledge of red flags that I did, so I knew he'd protect them. I didn't want to do that to Ralph though, so I'd hung on for as long as I could. I'd managed to make it this far, but this morning . . . I was different. The thought of them growing up without me did not consume me as much as my need to get away from Mike. I guess now I can sort of understand how Crickett, Mike Jr.'s real mom, had been able to walk away. I'm still selfishly on the fence about that. I understand her desire to get as far away from him as possible. To escape. That's the only word to describe what I was so desperate for: escape.

I called Cinnamon, one of my so-called "friends." I knew that she was sleeping with Mike, but she was also a mom with daughters. I told her that Lily was going to need to be picked up and that I was leaving soon enough.

I vaguely remember the paramedics. I do remember being at the hospital surrounded by people who were trying to shove shit down my throat and up my nose. I felt like I was in a scary movie. I was awake enough to feel what was happening. Strange hands were trying to hold me down while I fought them. I heard a voice say, "She's strong for a little one." Then I remember being woken up by a lady asking me if I was thirsty. *Shit yes, I'm thirsty!*

The next time I woke up was when I saw the black stuff on my hands and all down the front of my body. The joke was on me again. It wasn't water I'd been guzzling down earlier. It was coal in a liquid form. I couldn't taste it or smell it, but apparently, it had done what it was intended to do. I don't remember vomiting at all, but I must have. No more Flexeril, and I wasn't dead. Instead, I stayed in the ICU for a couple of days and then guess where I was off to next? Yep, the psychiatric unit. Just fucking great.

I was already in therapy with Mandi Jordan before this event. I was doing counseling, but I still didn't want to be alive. Counseling wasn't successful, not because Mandi wasn't there for me—because she was—but because the compounded trauma was just too much. But the Flexeril was a no-go. Instead, I was here, forced into more therapy while my kids were out there.

After I was admitted, Mike wasted no time at all. He went to the courts and filed an emergency protective order against me, because now he could officially say I was "crazy." Doesn't seem fair. In the protective order, he included the kids. Mike wasn't like me. When I'd had to get an order of protection against Mike, I was sad and scared and been intimidated into dropping it. For Mike though, this meant he was winning the game. It never bothered him to know how his actions might affect me. He made sure I was aware of his feelings and how wrong I was each time. Now, Mike thought he had an opportunity to dig the knife in as deep as he could, and he was quick to do so. As cold and smart as he is though, he still couldn't escape his own selfishness. Mike was still calling me while I was in the mental facility and coming to see me as well. He was violating his own order against me. I didn't actually find out about the protective order until sometime later. Who knows if it even went into effect?

While I was being held in this psychiatric unit, "Sturgis," the well-known biker rally, was coming to the next town over from us. That's Mike's jam, and he wasn't going to miss it. Unfortunately for him, he didn't know that I was in contact with Sarah. She told me that Mike had contacted her about coming for her three biological grandchildren so he could "take care of things around the house." Really, he needed them gone so he could attend Sturgis. Mike must not have informed Sarah that he'd gotten an order against me.

She told me of his call, and I begged her to do it and to keep them. I told her that I was getting out of the hospital and coming to be with my kids. Of course, Sarah—being the person that she is—was always up for doing something shady. Mike must also not have realized that giving Sarah my kids, and him contacting me, voided his protective order. Or maybe he did but thought everyone was too stupid, and he'd be able to pull off his plan before he was found out. Nonetheless Sarah came for my children, minus one, and took them back to Northwestern Oklahoma.

Mike got to attend his biker rally. I know this for a fact because he came to visit me in the mental hospital afterwards. I don't remember how many days later, but he came to see me and show me all the beads he'd gotten from Sturgis. He laughed and giggled about how much fun he'd had and all the things he'd witnessed. He told me of all the carefree women at the rally who'd ridden shirtless and all the boobs he "got to see."

There I was, sitting at a table on a psychiatric unit because only days before I'd attempted to end my own life. Don't think for one second that the nurses on that unit didn't see exactly what he was doing. They understood from that visit, and from all the phone calls they encouraged me to hang up from, exactly why I was in that room. Those nurses . . . I only wish I knew their names. I would find every one of them and thank them for saving my life. They weren't the ones that saved me from an overdose of medication, but they absolutely saved the rest of my life—the life of my children's mother. Along with group therapy, sessions with the doctor, and help from the right meds to keep me chill—because let's face it, at that time, I didn't have the mental capability to be chill—those nurses made me feel like a real person.

I might have been able to relax more and let the meds do their job if Mike wasn't still harassing me over the phone while I was suffering from a mental breakdown at just thirty years old. Those nurses knew I wasn't crazy, and they knew I had the potential to be somewhat normal if I weren't being tormented—maybe not completely normal but somewhat. They poured that faith into me. They helped me to get the courage to hang up on Mike. They helped me to understand that, if I went back into that house with him, I wouldn't survive. They helped me to gain the courage to tell Mike no. And finally, one day, I did.

Mike called me while I was there and told me that it was time for me to get back home and that I should do whatever I needed to do so that I could leave earlier. I was definitely doing what I should to get better, but I was definitely not going back into that house. I was really going away this time for good.

He flipped his lid when I told him I wasn't coming back. He said that I had to because of the kids . . . but he'd given the kids to Sarah, so they weren't coming back either. He couldn't do anything because he'd shipped them off as soon as he'd filed his protective order. He did it to himself, and that's probably what helped me the most. Mike was so pissed at me. In my voice, he could hear the change in me.

I'd scared myself by what I had done to myself because of Mike. I didn't want to die anymore, not when I was about to begin my exit from Mike Walker World. No matter how much he yelled, cussed, or threatened me, there wasn't anything he could do. He didn't know exactly what day I was leaving or when, and he didn't know where I'd go. He knew where the kids were roughly, but he didn't know where I was. Ultimately, he didn't want the kids. He just didn't want to lose his control over me. He wanted to control me and have me exist only to raise the kids. Mike needed someone to control.

I entered that hospital on September 6, 2010, began slowly manifesting a change, and walked out of there on September 24, 2010, someone a bit different. In the middle of the night, I was taken to a shelter for abused women and children. I stayed roughly two weeks before leaving for Northwestern Oklahoma, where my kids were waiting for me.

All the time I was in the hospital, and all the time I was in the shelter, Mike called and harassed Sarah, just like he did me. He cussed her just like he cussed me. He said the worst things to try and get her to break. It sucked for her, I'm sure, but it didn't do him any good, because she didn't know where I was either. She just knew that I was somewhere in Bartlesville. I'm glad she didn't know. As many times as she has thrown me under the bus, I feel like she would have caved, if she'd had the information he wanted. Sarah is spineless. I will say that I am glad she kept my kids during that time though. It was the least she could have done for any of us.

Did I mind that she was getting cussed by Mike? Not too much. It's not like I didn't think she deserved it. Yes, even though she allowed my children to stay with her, I'm still not going to put her up on a pedestal. Still . . . thanks, Sarah.

As much as I dreaded being there, and as much as I knew my children did too, by Halloween of 2010, the kids and I were back staying with Sarah and KD. As much I hated being around the two of them, even temporarily, that was my choice. That is what we had to do. That was our option at the time. My children and I were never going back to Mike. I was making sure of that this time. I immediately started filling out job applications.

Chapter 15

There was no way I was going to make us stay a single day in that house without making money to get us out. It didn't take long at all before I got employment at a local business and started saving money. Until then, KD put me to work for him so I could have daily cash before my taxable income. He had a very small tree-cutting team. Just a few men. When I arrived, they were in the middle of a decent-paying job, so he bought me a pair of work boots and some gloves. In that time, I learned how to split and stack wood for the winter. Of course, I didn't like doing it. I have little hands attached to a little body, so the work was very grueling for me, but like I said, there was no way I was wasting one day. Soon enough, I stopped stacking wood and started a minimum-wage job with taxable income. The kids and I moved out of Sarah's into an apartment where we stayed. I was so unimaginably happy when that day came! I'd never wanted us to spend a single day with Sarah and KD, and now we don't have to.

I can't describe how difficult it was, faking my way through every day with her. I can't tell you how hard it was not to lose my already fragile mind every time I had to hear KD's crude humor, which hadn't changed at all in those years. He was still the same man I remembered from the past. For the sake of my mental health, I couldn't be around them.

My kids would tell me about how Sarah and KD didn't show them any love in their time of need like loving grandparents but were cold instead. I didn't doubt it for one second. Why would I? I knew them. They were still the same rotten people they'd been when I was forced to live with them as a kid. That pushed me even harder to get us out of that place, and we did get out. We were our own happy little family. As happy as we could be. I tried my best to keep things as normal as possible for the kids, though I'm hanging my head as I write this. It is extremely difficult to be a single parent. My oldest son's father, Shannon, was hopeless. There was no way I could get clear conversation out of that guy let alone any financial support, guidance, or advice on raising our son. He'd dropped off the planet as soon as I'd taken our baby and left. It was easy for him to detach from David, so I knew not to ask anything of him. I knew he couldn't even take care of himself or the new children that he'd fathered after we left Arkansas. It was pointless for me to contact him. Do I wish I could have relied on Shannon to help me support David? Yes, of course I do, but there was zero point in trying.

Mike did not make my single parenting easy by any means, and of course, you knew that he wouldn't. Yes, I could have blocked Mike's number. Yes, I could have avoided him on social media. I could have chosen not to argue with him, the way he wanted me to, but I still did. I was scared to death of Mike, so why would I communicate with him, even from far away? All I can say is that, to a brain that functioned the way mine did at that time, it made sense. I knew that I never wanted to actually see Mike with my own eyes again, but the guilt I still carried was overwhelming. The guilt I felt for removing us from a toxic person was a real thing and heavy like a boulder. I was so convinced that the kids would hate me that I allowed them to talk with Mike over the phone. And of course, let's not forget that their brother, Mike Jr., still lived with Mike.

I allowed him to threaten me and run me down over the phone, though not to my face—no more of that. It made me cry so much knowing that Mike ran me down to anyone who would listen. I was so worried that people would call me a bad mom. I loved my children and was trying to be strong for their sake. Mike knew that he was easily able to play mind games with me. He knows that I'd grown up without my biological father and how much it had affected me. He knew that I had this notion in my heart that, if I'd had my own father growing up, maybe I wouldn't have experienced the things I had.

"How can you do that to your own daughter Lu? . . . She'll hate you for taking her dad away . . . You'll never be able to keep her safe, Lu . . . Without her dad, she'll end up just like you."

Why would I want my own daughter to end up like me? I'm so damaged, I would never want her to feel pain like I did. Mike knew exactly what to say to get me to break. Time and time again, from four hours away, I let Mike control my emotions, even if he could no longer control my body, trying to keep me in his grasp.

That December, in 2010, really was the end of my last physical year with Mike Walker. I never had to be touched by his hands again. We had settled down in Northwestern Oklahoma, where my kiddos and I slowly became part of a community. The boys did their best in adjusting to life at a new school. My little girl was still in daycare and had embraced her new little friends. I had a job, we had our own place, and life was okay.

Then over Christmas vacation in January of 2011, the kids and I ended up in the hospital with carbon monoxide poisoning. Something inside the central heat and air system in our apartment had broken, and the kids and I had breathed in the carbon monoxide as we slept. By "the kids," I mean my two biological sons, a child cousin, and a new friend the boys had just made. My daughter was actually spending the weekend with Mike. I'd been against him taking her, but now I am so thankful he did, because otherwise she would have been with us that night when I was woken up by a loud "thud."

It was the sound of the heaviest of the children hitting the ground after waking up and trying to stand up. I opened my eyes to see this boy lying on my hallway floor. As soon as I tried to stand up myself, I knew something was wrong. I couldn't stand up. I felt like I had just finished drinking the night away, but there had been no drinking at all. I was too dizzy and sick feeling to stand, so I crawled out of my bed to the child and tried to comfort him.

Next, I witnessed my own son walk towards me, taking only a couple of steps before also dropping to the floor. I watched David fall to the floor like a rock. I thought that I'd just watched him die in front of me. With those permanent memories etched into my brain, I didn't know what to do.

I left two kids laying in the hallway and crawled into the living area where the other two kids slept, calling to them in my mind. I heard my voice yelling out their names, telling them to please wake up, but they weren't waking up. Looking back, I can't honestly tell you that I was yelling out loud. I heard myself. I heard my own voice, but I don't think I had enough energy to actually yell. I was trying to wake those kids up, but nothing was happening. We were in a real-life nightmare. These kids and I were stuck in the same horrible dream.

Then I called Sarah. Why did I call her phone instead of dialing 9-1-1? I don't know. I'm sure there is some deep psychological reason why. Nonetheless, my feelings for her were set to the side when I crawled back to my phone; my first instincts were telling me to call my mother, the person for whom I have the deepest well of anger. When she answered, I said, "Something's wrong . . . We need help." All I remember after that was being slung over someone's shoulder and carried, calling for my kids still.

Eventually, I found myself in a community hospital, in bed, watching the hospital staff bring my kids in on stretchers. All I could possibly do was cry out to them and tell them how sorry I was for letting this happen. I was scared that the other parents would file a police report against me. I was scared, and I didn't know what was going on. I didn't want people to say that I hurt my kids. Most of all, I was afraid of what Mike was going to be able to do to me. What would he say? I was certain that, when he found out, he'd find a way to use this to take the kids from me.

We had to stay a couple of days in the local community hospital, but we all recovered well. Nobody hated me. It couldn't have been my fault. I still feel some guilt for the children harmed while in my care and, to this day and every day going forward, I know that the sound of that boy's heavy body hitting the ground is the only reason we didn't all die that night.

It was directly after that when Sarah, KD, and my younger siblings moved back to Eastern Oklahoma. Sarah didn't ask if the kids and I wanted to go back with them, and I didn't mind her going without us. I was grateful to her for keeping my kids while I was hospitalized while battling a mental crisis, and for her calling 9-1-1 that night. Other than that, I had no reason to miss her when she left. I didn't bother to help them pack. Other than my siblings going with them, I didn't care where they ended up. Is that wrong? I know that she called 9-1-1, but even total strangers would do that much for a person. The fact is that we were (and are) nothing to each other. I'd never felt any real comfort in her presence, not even growing up. I was finally getting to a place where I knew I would be fine without her. Does wanting a mom and not having one hurt? Yes. But sometimes we are better off without the people who should be the closest, which has proven true for me.

After that, I worked minimum wage for a while, and the State of Oklahoma helped me to provide food for the kids and myself. I did not receive any financial help from Mike, which you probably already assumed. Why would he do that? He felt absolutely no obligation to me or them. "You are the one that left, Lu . . . You are the one who destroyed our family, Lu . . . You are the one who took the kids from their dad, Lu . . . Guys do worse stuff to their wives, and they still tough it out, so the kids are on you, Lu . . ."

The only thing that fucking guy ever offered me was a hard time.

I worked at a local business, and through that business, I began to meet people who hired me for housekeeping services. The days I had off from my full-time job, I would do housekeeping in order to make extra money. Those side jobs allowed me to have cash on hand when my weekly paycheck ran out, which it did very quickly. The children and I lived paycheck to paycheck for a while until I was able to build up a housekeeping client list. That did add more work to my plate, but I needed the money.

At that time, I was making $7.25 an hour at my taxable-income job, which was not nearly enough to provide for three children alone, even working more than forty hours a week. I worked so much as a single woman to make ends meet for us, but we did it. We dealt with our everyday lives together. Me and my kiddos. We were doing it. Living in a new place, just me and the kids. We had the opportunity to start fresh and make a new life for ourselves without the negative influence of Mike. We were working on being happy. It hadn't been a way of life for any of us, so it took a while to adjust to "normalcy."

* * *

Fucking Mike. That guy didn't let up forever. Of course. After I left Bartlesville with the kids, he continued to take me back and forth to court, and the first judge granted custody of Jacob, the first child he and I had together, to his father (so that he could stay with Mike Jr.), and Lily was granted to me so that she could stay with David. Oh my God, I don't have to go into detail about how out of my mind I was when that happened. I cried so much and feared for Jacob's safety. I was scared for both his mental health and his physical wellbeing.

Mike is a psychopath. I didn't want Jacob to be subject to his physical and mental torture. This was a guy who'd once grabbed him and thrown him across the room by his hair for eating the last piece of Christmas candy. I swear in front of Jesus that he did that crazy shit, among a million other things that put our kids in harm's way. As an adult man, Jacob still remembers being thrown that day as a kid. That's the kind of behavior that makes me really want to hit Mike with a nailed-up two by four.

When the judge had made his ruling, Mike hopped around outside the Washington County Courthouse, literally jumping for joy, because he just knew Lily would be next to go with him. "You can't stop me, Lu! You're not strong enough to beat me!" He was taunting me as he watched me sob over my son.

I set an alarm on my phone and called Jacob every single day at 7:00 p.m. I never missed one day talking to my son because I needed to hear his voice. I needed to hear Jacob tell me every day that he was okay. During those calls, I also tried to talk to Mike Jr. By this time, it was working towards being hopeless though. Mike had completely convinced Mike Jr. that I'd ruined and broken up the family, that I didn't care for him, and that this was why I hadn't taken him with me, only his brothers and sister. Absolutely not the case. So, at that time, Mike Jr. wasn't interested in talking to me.

On one particular day, I called Jacob like I always did to talk about his day. Every day before this, I'd gotten the same response: "I'm fine, Mom. Everything is okay." But not this time. This time, I asked him the right question, and Jacob slipped up, revealing that he'd been instructed to give me certain answers. When I started asking more questions, I found out the truth: Mike had left Mike Jr., who was thirteen, and Jacob, who was ten, alone in the house while he took a plane to California to "check on his dying grandma." He'd left the boys alone in Oklahoma, and while he was in California, they would only be checked on by a current girlfriend of Mike's.

Jacob told me this, and I instantly lost it. It turns out Mike had been gone for nearly seven days before I found out. I immediately called the Washington County Sheriff Office, the Department of Human Services, and my attorney to let everyone know the situation and that I was on my way to pick up the boys and bring them back with me to Northwestern Oklahoma. While I was on the phone with the DHS, a supervisor told me that Mike was already being investigated for neglect of the boys, and that they would be going along with the officers who would be waiting for me when I arrived. Three hours later, my lawyer had paperwork ready for me to sign, allowing me to take Jacob. Unfortunately, since Mike Jr. is not my biological child, and legally, I wasn't even his stepmother because Mike and I had never married, he wasn't allowed to leave with me. Nobody was allowing me to take Mike Jr. anywhere, as neither of his biological parents—Mike and Crickett—were there to okay it.

Of course, Mike Jr. didn't know that. He knew only that Jacob left with me, and he had to go into DHS custody. Mike was notified right away that the police and the Department of Human Services had removed Mike Jr., and he was being taken into a foster-care situation until his could regain custody through the courts and DHS system. Mike was made aware that I had taken Jacob back with me. I assume that Mike hurried back to Oklahoma to help Mike Jr.

I know that this situation is how I was ultimately granted full custody of our two children together. I took my kids back home and raised them. Mike Jr. hasn't ever forgiven me for everything that happened. I don't expect that he will anytime soon, if ever. We both still have more years left to learn and grow though. If he were to ever let me hug him again, that would be the greatest day I can imagine. Maybe someday he will let me attempt to apologize for his bad memories of me, but so far, we've only had negative contact, so sadly, we don't stay in touch.

Mike continued to cuss me and use me as much as he could, and I allowed him. I had all three of my birth children together starting a different life, but the control Mike had over me was still lingering heavily. I still had so much guilt for taking the kids away from their brother. I was under extreme stress, still confused and worried about whether I was doing the right thing. I did my best to wear a strong, brave face, but Mike hounded me at every opportunity.

Although he had moved on to another female, who later birthed two more of Mike's daughters, he still harassed me about how I'd destroyed the family and how the kids would hate me for keeping him away. I knew I was being controlled, but I didn't see another way. My kids had already been through so much in their still very young lives. I didn't want them to hate me, which is exactly what Mike said would happen. And I fully believed him. I didn't get to know my biological father, and the pain from that was real. I still have animosity for Sarah for not allowing me to know him. I didn't want the same for my kids, and Mike knew it. He used my hurt from my father's absence against me. That's what a narcissist can do. So, all the way up until I met Will in 2015, I was actually sending Mike money to drive and see our kids.

Yes, I know, I know, I fucking know . . . I shouldn't have been doing that. Those of you who are reading this who know people like Mike understand why I was still bending for him. I was weak, and he is a master manipulator. I knew what he was doing. Mike would tell the kids that he was coming to visit them and then tell me that he needed gas money. If I said no, then it was my fault that the kids were unhappy, because they would think they'd get to visit their dad and then be disappointed. So, I'd wire him money. Then I'd have to give him money to take the kids for food, because there was no way I was going to be standing in the kitchen to feed Mike Walker! "Hey, Lu, what are you making us for dinner?" Not a fucking thing! Along with funding dinner, I would give him money for a hotel room, because he wasn't sleeping in my house.

Mike always planned this out. He did everything he could to take advantage of me and be as selfish as he possibly could, knowing that I would be in an impossible position in front of the kids. He came to my house penniless on purpose. Or, at least, he would tell me that he didn't have any money. Mike wanted me to cook for him, and he wanted to be in my house, to both of which was a huge fuck no! Instead, he gladly took my money.

"Well, Lu, if you can't help the father of your kids, then I'll just sleep here." No the fuck he wasn't. Then he needed money to get back to Bartlesville if I didn't want him stuck at my house. I should have called the police. I know. That son-of-a-bitch played me, preying on my emotions so many times. More times than I can tell you. And for all the guilt he laid on me for leaving Mike Jr., Mike never brought him with when he came to see the kids.

"Why would he want to see you, Lu. Look at what you did to him? You stole his family."

I literally made $7.25 an hour at my full-time job, plus housekeeping on the side, to keep the kids and me alive. If he couldn't hurt me physically, then he would do it financially. Mike knew that I had the inability to say no to him, at least until Will came into our lives. He helped me to make all of that stop. Thank you so much, babe.

Mike saw that Will wasn't going to let that shit happen to me anymore and immediately backed off. Just like that. I wanted to shotgun Mike in the face!! All the times I'd argued with him in my own home over money I didn't have to give him! All the times he'd made me feel guilty in my own home! All the times I'd had to defend myself when Mike still tried to come at me with sexual advances in my own home, and he only backs off when Will steps in?? I told you I didn't mean shit to Mike.

Just before Christmas, 2011, back before I ever met Will, I was on my way to Bartlesville to pick up Jacob and Lily from visitation from Mike. At that point, he had court-ordered visitations. I knew it was a bad call by the judge, but he didn't know Mike Walker yet. I left David with a friend of mine and took off to Eastern Oklahoma to retrieve my kids from Mike. You wouldn't think I'd have to drive all the way to Bartlesville for the kids, but I did. Mike wasn't having any of it. He was so pissed, and he hated me even more now than he had before. Why? Because I was slowly gaining strength and talked back to him a bit more without fear of what he would do. Don't get me wrong. I wasn't completely free from him mentally, not by any means, but I was working on myself more, and not living with him made it a little easier.

Mike despised me for it. "You're a liar, Lu . . . You are a user, Lu . . . People will see your true colors and hate you as much as I do, Lu . . ."

Maybe people would hate me and maybe people wouldn't, but from that point on, it wouldn't be Mike Walker hating me to my face.

On a dark, windy road somewhere between Pawhuska and Bartlesville, Oklahoma, I lost control of my 1985 Chevy Blazer and rolled it, time after time. It was 9:30 p.m. in December, so it was pitch black outside. I was alone in my vehicle. The driver behind me told the highway patrol officer that I'd only been doing 55 mph when I'd suddenly lost control and swerved. I don't know what happened. I didn't reach over to mess with the radio, I didn't touch my cell phone, and I sure as hell didn't fall asleep behind the wheel. I was awake the entire time.

When my Blazer left the road, I panicked. I didn't know why I was suddenly heading for the ditch! All I knew to do was something I'd once heard Mike say: "Try not to overcorrect." I guess I didn't do something right though, because when I got back to the road, I was all over the place. I couldn't get my Blazer to correct itself. So, I just let go of the wheel. I really did. Not like in a "Jesus Take the Wheel" moment. It was more like an "I'm so scared and don't know what to do" moment.

I took my feet from the pedals, let go of the wheel, and rolled my Blazer several times. Afterwards, as I sat on the ground, in shock as to what had happened, a state trooper told me that my seatbelt had broken, and I must have fallen out a side window while I was in the air. When my Blazer had stopped rolling, it was upside down only feet away from me.

As I was falling out one of those side windows, I'd been completely aware of what was happening. The only thing I could think to do in order to save myself was tuck myself into a ball and hope for the best—and the best actually happened. I hadn't died. Again. It seemed like it was only minutes before an ambulance arrived but as I had just fallen out of a rolling car, I wasn't so clear about time. I remember someone being there immediately, even before the ambulance, asking me if I was okay. I'm sure it was a woman's voice. She was surely in the car behind me. What a story the people in that car got to tell when they got home!

Then there were lights from the ambulance and police. I was looked over by paramedics and seemed physically fine to them.

Of course, I still needed to be carried off to the hospital for X-rays. My vehicle wasn't so lucky as it was absolutely smashed and upside down in the road. None of the X-rays showed any visible damage. All I had was a superficial scratch on my lower back. Thank you once more to God. While at the hospital, they looked at my license and saw that I didn't live nearby. The officer asked me who my closest contact would be, and since I was right outside Bartlesville when I'd crashed, sadly, that contact was Mike.

Of course, I had to be just minutes outside Bartlesville when I crashed—where my kids were expecting me to pick them up, probably at any moment. So, the staff had to call Mike and tell him what had happened. They told him to just hang on to the children, and I'd be there as soon as possible. Someone came from Nortwestern Oklahoma, to get me. We picked up the kids and went back home. The only thing Mike had to say was, "I prayed this would happen, Lu. I don't want you driving around in a Blazer I built for you if we aren't together."

Fuck you, Mike! I still didn't die, as much as you wished I would have.

Once back in Northwestern Oklahoma, I sat back, took a minute, and actually thanked God for not allowing me to die so many times in a row. I thanked God for not allowing me to be killed or kidnapped as a child when I'd had no guidance or supervision and could have been so many times. I thanked God for allowing me to keep my children through many times of mental anguish and distress. I thanked God for allowing us to be safe and able to start a new life. I thanked God for allowing me to have the strength to stand alone physically . . . while he stood by my side.

Chapter 16

There was a woman's conference at a small church in town. Tara, a single mom like myself with whom I had also become friends (through our daughters), said, "Come with me to the conference, and if you don't like it, you don't have to stay." I went to that conference, which was completely out of my comfort zone. I didn't know a single person in that building, but by the time the afternoon was over, I had made a whole new family of women.

This introduction to new people was hardly easy at first. I had a fear of people in general and had never been involved in anything so close-knit, especially not in a church. It was an uncomfortable journey out of my shell, but I knew I had to keep going. This was a place where my kids and I needed to be. I didn't know Christine Cain before the conference that afternoon, but by the time I had finished hearing her speak, I realized there were other people like me. She had overcome so much too, and because of her, that day I knew that I could do even more than I was doing. I felt like we were the same person.

From that day forward, for the sake of my mental health, no matter how exhausted I was by the end of the week, I made sure that the kids and I were sitting in that church building. I wouldn't let what had already happened twice happen again. I couldn't lose it. I had to keep it together. I couldn't let my kids watch me fail them again.

My therapist Mandi Jordan had told me, time and time again, to find a church home. I got so sick of hearing her say that to me. At that time, Mike was taking his last emotional jabs at me. He was relentless. Whenever she suggested finding a church family, I'd think, *How can me going to church make Mike stop being his tyrannic self?*

But it wasn't for Mike, was it? It was for me. Mandi, you were right the entire time.

Although I felt like I stuck out like a sore thumb, although I thought they were all looking at me oddly, although I was afraid to open my mouth and sing out loud because I thought I would draw attention to myself (like those songs weren't meant for me to sing), and although I felt like they could see all my dirty secrets like a bright-colored shirt covered in filth, I still made us go sit in that church house. I was doing my best to single parent. I worked hours far beyond what I had the strength to do, and I was exhausted to the core.

In a separate conversation I was having with Tara, the lady who'd first invited me to the women's conference, I was talking to her about how much I wished I could purchase a home for my kids. I felt I needed a foundation for us, a place that belonged to us, so we'd never have to face the possibility of homelessness. I didn't need anything fancy, just something with walls and a roof. Something I could build for us. Being the friend that she is, Tara took in a deep breath and said, "Well, I do know a place." She took me to the house, and as soon as we pulled up the drive, I could see why she'd been a bit hesitant.

There was a man there in the yard, cleaning up what looked like years of garbage. I took a deep breath and thought to myself that I had absolutely nothing to lose. I put on my bravest face and approached him. We talked about me being a single mother, about my income status, and about how, by this time, I had been in this town nearly three years and had built for myself a reputation for being an honest, hard-working lady who was as good as her word. He needed to sell, and I desperately needed something to purchase.

By the end of that month, I was signing an agreement for a house-buying option. That was in December of 2013, three years after our flight from Mike Walker. Thank you, Tara. You are the person God put in my path to lead me through those church doors. You had enough faith that I could turn anything into a home that you drove me to that corner house that day. Thank you.

I still ask myself why I tried to include Sarah in this event—not so much in my life but I still wanted to tell her about what, for me, was a moment of success. I wanted her to be proud of me. I wanted to show her how much I had achieved. I was a single-mom property owner! I'm sure I thought that this was what would finally make her proud. Not the single-mom part or the still-making-minimum-wage part, which I was still working on. But I had signed a contract to own my own piece of property. How exciting, right? I was wrong, and it had been wrong of me to expect anything from her.

The house needed to be completely gutted. In my mind, I thought that this could be something she and I could work on together. I thought that perhaps she might take a weekend and join with me in building a foundation for her family. Maybe she could pick up a paintbrush and join in on building a life for her grandkids. No. Neither her nor KD had any interest in being a part of it in any way. Not once did she ask me if there was something she could do to help me. That's fine though. I didn't ask her for her help. Whatever. She was still driving her own wedge between us, just as she'd done my entire life. Why would they change now that I was an adult?

Instead of help from my own mother, Sarah, I got it from Poppa and Jenni, a couple I had met in my new community who'd seen me trying to manage being a single mom. They saw my struggle to be the sole provider for three children and took us under their wings. They made us family. For once, I was able to feel a sense of relief. For me, they are "friends to the end" and always have been. They were so proud of us when they came to see our fixer-upper home. They were so proud of us for working on a future and not just giving up. Poppa and Jenni were there for us through the entire remodeling process. I would have struggled even more if it weren't for them being by my side. Being a single, low-income mother made it difficult for me to afford renovations, but again, Poppa and Jenni were there watching out for me. Jenni, I love your friendship. I love you. It's partly because of you that I have a backbone today. You have lifted me so many times when I was at my lowest. I love everything you are to me.

In 2015, God came through for me again when I met my husband, someone who saw something in me that not too many people did: softness and beauty trapped under the stress of life-long abuse. It didn't matter to him that I had children, or that I was twelve years older than him, or that my entire life was under construction. Within months, Will asked me to be his wife, even after witnessing me be triggered and going into a violent PTSD episode. He sees my flaws and doesn't ignore me when life gets me down. He wants to be my companion. Sadly, life getting me down happens more often than I would like to admit.

It's hard for my husband to live with a wife who has suffered so much trauma. It's sometimes difficult for him to deal with or understand me when I'm in a fit of craziness spawned by PTSD. I'm still letting God help me through that. Thank you, Will, for doing your best to love someone like me. I know it's beyond tough. Thank you for being here. I love you.

* * *

It's 2021 now. I will be forty-one this year. I have been sexually assaulted numerous times. I've been beaten up by both men and women. I've been humiliated, frightened, terrorized, and sad beyond despair. I've been heartbroken, hospitalized, abandoned, lonely, and left unprotected.

I haven't had to be touched by Mike Walker's hands in ten years. I haven't had him bringing girls to my house to try and fight me in seven years. I haven't gotten a threatening phone call from Mike in five years. I still fight with him mentally. Sometimes I still think I see him out of the corner of my eye, even though I know he's in prison now. I have been on clinically prescribed PTSD medication since 2010 and still have to fight to keep Mike from consuming my thoughts or causing me triggers, even though it has been eleven years and he can no longer get to me physically.

A person might think it would be the rapes that haunt me the most. And yes, they have impacted my self-worth, which is something that I'm still working through. Maybe the lack of a nurturing bond and the neglect by my own mother could have impacted me so deeply that I'll forever miss out on that part of love. Being physically attacked by my alcoholic first husband for four years may have also played its part in my deep-rooted unease.

But none of that is more chilling than Mike's angry eyes boring into mine, the sound of his voice, and his terrifying threats. Those impacted me most. I frequently apologize to my husband because my frustrations with Mike are still an underlying issue for me. It hurts him, but he tries so hard to understand. I hate my PTSD, but at the same time, it drives me to do the best for my family by breaking generational cycles of destruction. I hate my PTSD, but without it, I might not be so brave.

After several X-rays and MRIs over the past two years, I have been diagnosed with degenerative disc disease in the cervical portion of my spine, which I will have surgery for in the hopes of repairing damage. I have three bulging discs in the lower lumbar portion of my back that send shooting pains down into my legs. I saw a neurologist and went through several tests for that as well. From those results, I know that the shooting pains down my arms and into my hands, as well as the numbness in my fingers, is caused by ulnar neuropathy in both of my elbows. All of these things cause me extreme nerve pain from my neck all the way down to my toes.

After visits with a rheumatologist, I have been diagnosed with psoriatic arthritis as well as osteoarthritis, both of which cause me deep aching pains in the joints of my body. I have to see a specialist for each of these painful issues, and each of these issues cause more stress to an already uneven lady. Along with the conditions and related specialists come a series of prescription meds that take their chemical toll on my system.

Am I happy that, after thirty years, I finally got away from people using me for abusive conduct only to grow older ten years earlier than I should have? Not really. I still need my body for so many more years. Am I happy that I finally escaped Mike but still think I hear his voice all these years later? Not really. It makes me jumpy and paranoid. Am I happy that I have no choice but to wear a mask that hides my tears from chronic pain? No, it makes me depressed. These reasons plus many more are why I still have to take meds for diagnosed PTSD and depression. But am I happy to be alive?

YES! Absolutely!

I now have two adult sons. My relationship with David, my oldest, is vague to say the least. He went off on his own life adventure and chooses to blame me for the negativity spawned from his life choices. He has three children, one which my husband and I adopted, one that was adopted by another family, and the third is safe with her own mother. My second son, Jacob, suffered mental-health issues from the trauma of watching Mike and I scream at each other and physically fight over him as a child.

Both of the boys, in their own way, suffered from my PTSD and depression while I single-parented them. One went out into the world, acting out with no regard for other people, and he's now constructed his own tangled web; and the other developed social-anxiety issues and stays close to home with a fear of going out into the world. I still have my thirteen-year-old little girl, Lily, of whom I'm extremely overprotective, to a fault at times. Mike told me I couldn't protect her, but he was wrong because I do. I've acted a fool, gotten into arguments, and even blocked people from our lives just to protect her. I never want the same thing to happen to her that happened to me.

Her life is different than mine though. I'll die fighting to break toxic cycles in our family. I try so much to pour everything I can into her, again sometimes to a fault. I want Lily to hear me fighting for her. I never want her to have to wonder if I was there. I'm always right here. My worry and concern for her has made for some pretty intense outbursts on my part. These are called triggers, and they come from trauma. I can't make some triggers disappear, but I can try to control them with therapy, church, and medication. Sometimes my triggers are stronger than others and are harder to control, and their frequency changes as well. I have to continually work on myself.

I have to remember and understand that Lily is not me. She will be so much better, and I'm sure she'll be great at everything. I told you I have three grandchildren fathered by David. The oldest grandson was adopted by my husband and I when he was just shy of a year old. He calls Will and I "Mom and Dad." It does affect me. This is my fourth completely different life with a fourth completely different family. I have memories that nobody else has. I can't really talk about anything that happened in my three previous families and lives, because nobody from my current family was there. I just keep them to myself. It doesn't feel to me like I've been alive long enough for all these events, people, and lives I've been a part of, but I have. I've got forty-one years' worth of real memories.

I'm happy to be alive, because not too long ago, I did for myself what Sarah should have done for me as a girl. My husband drove me to the Blackwell Police Department, and I discussed with J. Brewer the same thing I have had to say out loud in front of my therapist Staci so many times. Alvie Wilson raped me as a toddler, and he's still alive, living in East Oklahoma. I told J. Brewer, in detail, what Alvie did to me and that he has been known to work at nursing homes around helpless people. It took me an entire lifetime to gain the courage to do that. I had to be "adult Lu" and tell the gruesome story about "toddler Lu," because she had no child advocate of her own.

Sadly, and to my disbelief, I was completely dismissed. Yes, the officer listened to my story but found it hard to believe that I would wait until I was forty to come forward. He found it hard to believe that Sarah wouldn't have reported it. He found it hard to believe because I could only recall one instance of Alvie assaulting me. He kept repeating, "So it only happened once when you were four?" He finds this all hard to believe because he doesn't understand how the traumatized brain works.

After speaking with Brewer and a more-local officer of the law, I've come to understand that, because Sarah never filed any charges against anyone, and she didn't report any of my sexual assaults, there is nothing on file anywhere that would back up my stories. It's like the assaults never happened. It has been too many years, and there is no evidence besides my very own memory box.

There is nothing in the law books that would allow me to bring charges against Alvie myself, because of course, it's been too long. I can't now, as an adult, take ANY of my abusers to court, because Sarah failed to provide protection before or after. No documentation.

I have faith that Alvie has not lived a good life. One of the hardest things for me to face as a human is now being an adult, knowing exactly where he is, and not being able to go to him. But I'm not scared anymore.

On April 28, 2021, I reached out to James Wallace on messenger. He was eager to talk until I told him that I remembered every second of him taking my virginity. He then quickly told me how bad his substance abuse was, that he was sorry for my pain, and then he blocked me on social media. I am sure that he feels slightly paranoid now. I'm sure he wonders, in the back of his mind, when the police are coming for him. Don't worry, James; it's been too long or else they would be. It doesn't give me any closure really, but it does make me chuckle slightly to think of him fearing prison. James knows I'm alive, and that I remember. Maybe he reached out to Sarah. I don't know. Anything is possible with predators.

I'll never forget James, because like the rest of them, he took a significant piece of me not once but twice. The first time, he took my virginity, and the second time, he took a piece of my heart and my uterus. I haven't shared it with you yet, but James Wallace did come back to see me once more before we left for Arkansas. That time I was almost fifteen years old, and the visit ended with me in the emergency room having a miscarriage and a DNC. If you don't know what that is, you can easily look it up. This miscarriage was just another thing that my body was forced into. I immediately pushed it into the back of my brain. I tried to act like it wasn't happening. I never wanted to live that moment. At almost fifteen, it was something that had never crossed my mind.

When I woke from my DNC, I turned my head and looked to my right. In a clear plastic solo cup, sitting on a shiny steel table, was my first baby. I'm so sorry to you, baby, but it was better you be in Heaven than try to live life beside me. I love you, baby, and I'll never forget you.

Once again, Sarah was fully aware of what happened and why. Being my "mother," she had to put her signature down in order for me to be treated. That bitch had to put her name down on paper. She had to admit to her guilt with that signature. Fucking bitch.

You'd think something like that would be traumatic for a girl. It was. My heart, my mind, and my body were all being ravaged by all sorts of different pains all at once. I'd just seen my first baby, but it wasn't alive, only a blob small enough to fit in a solo cup. Sarah acted like it didn't happen, because she didn't want to talk about it, or more so, she didn't want to have to tell me she was sorry. I just let my baby go to Heaven and put another memory in the box.

When I attended Johnnie's funeral, I'd asked about Mel. Where was he? I was older and felt like I was ready. In reality, it's good for me that he wasn't there. In late September of 2018, someone sent me a link, which took me directly to a news article with Melvin Hyde Jr.'s obituary. He had died from a gunshot wound to the belly. As I read on, it said that he had opened the front door of his residence and outside stood a man with a shotgun who'd pulled the trigger. The man who shot Mel dead was also a registered sex offender. And just like that, the guy who'd coined the phrase "If she's old enough to bleed, then she's old enough to breed" would not be raping any more children. He would no longer get to molest, embarrass, or ruin the life of another child.

Robert H. is dead now too. A shit diet and diabetes did him in. He died in a pretty dreadful way. He had a stroke and hit the floor while he was standing in his kitchen. The ambulance came and took him to the hospital. Turns out his wife at the time had a way better notion of who he was than I did. I had already been warped by him, but she was a mom and a woman who saw past his bullshit. Luckily for everyone, she didn't stop him from eating himself to death. After he arrived by ambulance, his lab work said his blood sugar was at a thousand. Robert lay in that hospital bed and had mini stokes in the back of his brain until he died nine days later. I felt bad for him at first and carried on with Brenda about how she didn't help him. Now though, after years of therapy, I understand her better. Brenda, I owe you an apology. I could even say thank you.

Who knows what happen to Dan? He was the guy Sarah dated right after she and KD divorced. Another abuser of mine, and my childhood "drinking buddy". I'm sure he's near death by now if not already gone. He was such an alcoholic that I'm assuming it has done him in by now. As for Uncle Kirby, as I mentioned before, you can google his name (Kirby Logan Archer) and read that he's still in prison for stealing a boat and killing all four people on board because he was trying to escape the police for charges of larceny and child molestation, which had been reported by yet another mother who cared more for her child than Sarah did. Nope, not a good life for that guy either. You can't fuck little kids while you are in prison. Sucks for him.

Shannon Beasley has a shit life. He never chose to make anything of himself, for himself or his many children and grandchildren. He never managed to keep a job or own anything for himself. He never learned to work or save money like most normal people (and even some abnormal people) do. He never had his own place to live or drove his own car. To this day, he has no ambition to be anything more than a bum. Shannon is three years older than me and has nothing to show for his time on earth but dirt in his pockets. David didn't need a person like Shannon in his life. I'm glad I took my son and left Arkansas. I'm sure Shannon doesn't have many years left either. Of course, I say David didn't need a person like Shannon and his negative influence, but David didn't benefit from our lives with Mike either.

I raised David alone from the time he was twelve until he moved out when he turned seventeen. I did try so very hard to be a good mother to David, though I expected things from him, with him being the oldest child. Perhaps my "nurture" in this case wasn't enough to beat "nature"? I did what I thought was right while dealing with single-mother difficulties. I tried to instill moral values and responsibility into David, but he still chose the path of his father.

I'm guessing that Paul Archer, Sarah's fourth husband, is still alive and still an ignorant lazy-eyed fuck like he was every day I knew him. During Covid quarantine, he actually had the nerve to send Ralph and I Facebook friend requests. Ralph's reply is his own to tell, but mine was an emoji that in most parts of the world (if not all) represents the phrase "Fuck you." Apparently, he didn't get any smarter as he got older, because he didn't think those requests through. Always remember to treat children with kindness, Paul. Most kids are smart and don't forget. Some kids are traumatized and can't. Those kids turn into adults who got beef. I hope I never see that guy's face ever again. It would be very different than last time.

Chapter 17

As I sit here, putting words on paper, Mike sits in an Oklahoma prison for at least the next eight years. He was caught attempting to burn down the house where two of his own daughters and their mother lived. He only went to prison for attempted arson. During the time he was out on bail for this attempted arson charge, he set fire to another home, and that one burned to the ground. This time there was a woman in that house, and she died in the fire. Now because of the McGirt vs Oklahoma ruling, the State of Oklahoma had to drop the murder charges, and he'll now be charged in a federal court. I guess that story is still to be continued. I shake my head at you, Mike. Just know that.

I now make my daughter's life as normal as possible in order to keep her from becoming a statistic. Will helps me with that. He came into our lives with open (and at times unsure) arms and has done his very best to fill that massive void you left open. We are offering Lily a normal life. Not crazy. Normal. I say this with a full smile, because normal is good. She doesn't have to be a Mike Walker victim, and she won't ever be. We protect her from people like him.

Listen, I'll let Mike go, but before I do, I'll tell you one good thing he did for which I can only give him credit. Not acknowledging it would be dishonest. Mike is the only reason I got to meet my actual biological father—the one thing I wanted so much, the day that I daydreamt about as a kid. Mike made that day happen for me. Of course, he held it over my head enough times that I could never forget it was him. "If it weren't for me, Lu, you wouldn't even know who your own dad is. I did that, Lu."

It was back in 2003 or 2004, when we lived in Blue Eye, and Mike was having his way with Cindi, and maybe he was feeling some sort of remorse? Guilt maybe? I doubt it, of course. I'd like to think he did it for me and only me, but I know Mike too well. He doesn't have remorse or guilt. It just isn't humanly possible for him. Maybe he thought that, if he did this for me, it would be enough to trap me for good—you know, in case I thought about leaving. More than likely, I think that he was just curious. Whatever the reasoning, it was Mike who made it happen.

Of course, ever since realizing that none of the men Sarah had in my life was my actual father, I had wanted my real dad. I had made up this tale in my mind that he was out there somewhere, just for me. That someday he'd hug me and call me his princess. He'd give me a dad hug. I just knew that, once I got to my dad, I would be absolutely free from suffering. My dad was my imaginary friend. As time went on though, and my life just became more and more toxic, I put thoughts of finding my dad on the backburner. He was important to me, but I never thought I would actually get to see his face. I had really given up. All I had was a name: Robin Hardridge. No face, no memory, no idea. All I had was a name that Betty, a friend of Sarah's, let slip out one day.

Sarah was never going to tell me, so I had to beg her friends. I started that when I was little, asking people questions about who I looked like. Betty would always touch me on the face when I was a kid and say, "You look just like him." She never would say who though, until one day . . . when she did. Maybe she thought I was old enough to know. Thank you, Betty. If it wasn't for you saying his name just that once, I would have never known.

It only took that one time. I held onto his name forever. I locked that name away in my memory box, never to let it escape. I'd bring him up to Sarah here and there in conversation, and each time she'd act like she didn't know what I was talking about. She didn't talk "real dad" stuff with me. She tried to convince me that my father was Robert H., remember? But I knew in my heart I didn't belong to him.

Well, I found out why she didn't talk about it many years later. It's because Sarah had had an affair with a married man, Robin Hardridge, and BAM, she had me. She was seventeen at the time, and he was ten years older than her, with a wife and some kids. She said it only happened once. We will all be the judge of that. She had just married Robert H., so she tried pulling him off as my father, even though she'd left that part blank on my birth certificate. *What the fuck kind of sense do you make, Sarah?* That ignorant bitch didn't have a clue what she was doing. Anyways, I don't have a clue if Robin knew that I existed. That's another thing that I thought I'd never ever know.

So, when I was twenty-three or twenty-four, Mike did some digging on the internet from the name I gave him. He found a man by the same name, and by studying our features, we determined that this man must be him. I met my biological father for the first and last time somewhere around the summer of 2005. That was the only day that I ever laid eyes on my father. He didn't know who I was until we were introduced. I didn't see him again until his funeral in 2014. From that loss, I gained four half-brothers, a half-sister, many nieces, nephews, and extended family. I look like all of them. *They* are who I look like. It's okay, and I'm okay.

* * *

Sadly, both Sarah and KD are still alive. They are still living their worst sack-of-shit lives up on a dirt hill in their run-down trailer shack. The both of them are old and broken down now. Age and time has not been good to them, which is completely their own fault, of course. She is still the exact same woman I was forced to grow up with. If you walk into her home today, you will still see animal shit and garbage on the floor. There are still piles of dishes in the sink and on the countertops, and you'll still see shit in the fridge with mold growing on it. You'll still see piles of dirty laundry strewn about and mold, dirt, and disgust on every surface of the bathroom. It remains uncomfortable and uneasy in their house.

Sarah still has the same hopeless, lazy, low-functioning mentality that she's always had, and KD is still the same brass, vulgar, perverted son-of-a-bitch he always was, but now they're just old. I've been through a lot with Sarah and KD and because of Sarah and KD. We all have. Myself and my siblings. Sarah specifically let me down as a mother so many time that it's impossible to count them.

The last time I saw Sarah or KD in person was August 1, 2020. It was a Saturday. Just days before that, Sarah had been harboring my second grandson and his mother while the rest of the world—including me—were looking for him, scared to death. Being that the relationship dynamic between myself and my grandson's mother is also bad, I was scared that she had him somewhere in another state and that I would never see him again, as that's what I was led to believe. (He has now been adopted by a beautiful family)

I found out at some point that this wasn't the truth, and they had both been staying at Sarah's house for who knows how long. Someone in the family thought I should know and finally told me. No way did I want my grandbaby in the same house with Sarah and KD! And why hadn't Sarah brought this to me right away? She knew how worried I was for that little boy. He was in a bad situation, and I was afraid for where he might be and who he could be with. Yet she'd kept it from me. Sarah had them right there in front of her and had never once reached out to tell me that she could physically see my grandson. I'd cried to her about how worried I was for him, and she'd kept his whereabouts a secret. That was the final act of betrayal, Sarah. No more.

On August 1, 2020, my husband drove me to Sarah's house, three hours away, where I had called a sibling meeting. Ralph, DJ, and I were there, and with our spouses, sat in a circle as I said the words I needed to say to Sarah and KD. My sister Sandra wasn't there. She didn't try to be there. She said she was stuck working. So be it. We sat in a circle, and everyone listened while I brought it all out into the open. Everyone listened as I confronted them with forty years' worth of abuse, neglect, and betrayal, all of which she had forced on us. I confronted her about all the sexual abuse that we never received counselling for, and how our relationships had suffered from it, mine in particular. I explained how her lack of care for us led to my constant abuse at school and ultimately led to me not caring about my education. I confronted her and KD about what they'd allowed to happen to my sister, and how she'd also had no form of therapy. I also confronted them about the hardest thing that I felt had to come out.

It wasn't Alvie. It wasn't how she never stepped in to stop physical abuse. It wasn't how she'd birthed us and then left us to fend for ourselves. It was the day she'd come into my room and invited me to do sex things with them. It was about the day I had to ask her to leave my room before I broke down in tears from heartache. I asked them to explain to us as a group what the thought process had been that night, and as I fully expected, they denied the whole thing. Well, he denied it. Sarah never said a word.

Now, I have come pretty far mentally. I've had heartbreaks, breakdowns, and episodes that have landed me in a psychiatric unit on suicide watch. From all that, I personally feel that I am thriving to the fullest of my capabilities, all things considered. I have had therapy for most of the past ten years, and with that therapy, combined with sitting in a church room on Sundays, I feel like I'm stronger than I was before. I have overcome some stuff that maybe a lot of people never could have—or might have struggled with even more before they were able to reach a place of peace. I have gained so much courage in the past ten years, and I know that because I was able to talk about this specific situation in front of my brothers and their wives.

This is KD's response, verbatim: "There is no way she would have done that. I've been trying to get this woman to have a threesome with me for years, and she would never, so I know she wouldn't have asked you that." He said that to my face in front of everyone.

I felt like he could have come up with a better denial if I would have given him more time to lie. That stupid man didn't think that I would remember that day in the past, and he sure never thought I'd have the guts to bring it up to him, especially in front of other people. I'd put him on the spot, and he sounded completely stupid in his response. It wasn't good enough for me, but ultimately, it would have to be. His foolish response, and his lack of any kind of credibility or remorse, proves his guilt well enough. I'll get nothing more than that.

I'm sorry, DJ. I'm sorry that you had to hear all those things I needed to say about your father. I am sorry that I put you in the middle of such a fire storm that day, but it had to happen. You have to know that he abused Sandra, Ralph, and myself. The abuse was different for each of us, but it came at his hands, nonetheless. KD caused me so much damage that, to this day, my own husband suffers from my flashbacks of torture. Sarah had basically nothing to say. She just sat smugly in her chair and allowed me to talk about all these things she had done, or failed to do, right in front of her and everyone else, with zero remorse.

The entire hour that I sat and confronted her with one horror story after another, she sat there so calmly. She didn't shed a tear when I talked about Mel's unnoticed sexual assault of me and my sister. She didn't seem bothered when I finally, on this day, told her of Robert H. and what he had done to me. She didn't seem even remotely upset when I talked about Alvie. She only stared right back at me, cold and callous. She never even broke eye contact.

Only when I made her apologize to Ralph for shipping him off with Kirby Archer, with no concern for his safety, did she take her eyes off me. That bitch didn't shrug. She didn't have any sort of redness or watering in her eyes, as you would expect of a mom having to listen to her daughter tell stories and make accusations that would make any parent shudder. Not Sarah. Not even one tear. At one point, after she listened to me lay into her, she did try to give me a throw-up-your-arms hug, and I told her how fast she'd get beaten if she touched me. She rescinded the offer.

The only words that Sarah had to say were not of comfort. They were only excuses. She followed my stories with: "I didn't know about that . . . If you would have told me then, I could have done something . . . You wouldn't let me help you . . ."

The only thing she didn't have an off-the-top-of-her-head excuse for was why I'd never been offered any counseling when I told her James had taken my virginity, or why Ralph never got any counseling, support, or even a question of concern when it came out that "Uncle Kirby" was a child molester! Of course, she never had any questions for him because the answers would all be the result of her own neglect. She's such a fucking coward.

Sarah didn't do shit for me either, but in that moment, I was wrapped up in what she hadn't done for Ralph or Sandra. To this day, that woman does nothing but make their lives harder.

The point of that day wasn't to gain an apology. I knew I wasn't getting one. Closure would have been fantastic, but I hold onto faith that my closure will come with her passing. The point of that day was to bring to the surface who those people really were and the wreckage they had caused. I told the truth of who they were all those years ago, and how they were the exact people now, sitting in front of me, only in older shells. They were the grandparents to my nieces and nephews, and both of them were sex offenders. It was time everyone knew the truth.

The day was about exposing them, about releasing all the pent-up animosity I hold for them, cleansing my soul, saying goodbye to one of the foulest human beings I ever had the misfortune to know, and telling her to her face that she was no longer my mother. I said goodbye to Sarah and KD as I watched their jaws drop, knowing I was free. I'd voiced loudly, to a circle of eight adults, that those two evil humans were dead to me. On the day those two fucks finally die, I don't want to know, because I don't care that much.

Neither of them is allowed to look at my face again in life. They are uninvited from my family. They are evil people who forced us to be part of their cycle of destruction, their generational malfunction, and their world of abuse that we didn't ask to be in and had no other option but to survive. The day she dies, I know I'll finally be able to feel the freedom.

* * *

So, here I am on this day in my life. All the shit I just told you is 100 percent the honest to God truth. None of it is stretched, false, or misleading. If anything, I didn't tell you all of it because none of us have that much time. If people who meet me haven't read this book, or haven't finished reading it, they would think I was just a regular, normal person—a little rough around the edges maybe, but for the most part, they'd think I'm normal. That is because I am fully aware of my mental illness. I know that's it's there, and I don't deny it—or at least I try not to. I do my very best to learn new lessons, stay on top of my medications, stay in church, keep in contact with my therapist, and try like hell not to let PTSD control my life. I'm learning not to make excuses for it anymore but address it instead so I can work on being normal.

If I used the contents of this book as an excuse and acted out because of all the negative things I've been through, I'd be a monster. I'd be just like Mike and the others. Nobody would understand, my actions would be completely my own fault, and I'd be labeled "CRAZY." That doesn't seem very fair, does it? Other people go through the same shit I did—maybe not so much or maybe even worse—and they don't make it out okay. The cycle of abuse trickles down to other family members. Children come from abusive homes and don't talk about it—they don't talk about it; they can't talk about it; they don't know how to talk about it; they don't have anyone to talk about it with; or nobody cares enough to pay attention, notice, and help.

So, guess what happens? Those people become the odd ones out. They get labeled strange, dirty, slutty, mental, no good, or whatever other negative label a person can get stamped with that makes them "less than worthy" . . . and it could all be avoided if someone just took a second to ask why: Why does that kid sit alone every day? Why is that little girl so jumpy? Why does that mom walk with her head hung so low?

All of us are guilty, in one way or another, of ignoring signs and red flags instead of speaking out. All of us are guilty of putting a label on someone instead of being brave enough to learn the truth. All of us are guilty of looking the other way.

Learn to stop doing that. Have compassion and learn how to gently ask uncomfortable questions. You just might save someone's life. Even more importantly, learn not to judge a book by its cover. Some book covers are shiny, smooth, solid, and appealing to the eye, while inside, the story is pure evil. Some covers have deep cuts and slashes, are repeatedly taped together, and are masked by yet another cover. After a while, that cover becomes less appealing to the eye but the story inside is genuine.

Pay attention.

Love,

Lucy

About the Author

Having been through so much in her past, and finally living in a loving and secure present, Lucy Henson is all too aware of how dangerous it is to keep our traumas to ourselves, hidden in the shadows of shame or regret. Only by speaking out can we raise awareness of the long-term effects of abuse … and break the cycles of violence and neglect that crush the hopes, dreams, and potentials of one generation after another.

She hopes that by sharing her story, as difficult as it has been, others will be inspired to speak out about their own experiences, learn to watch for signs of it in others who might be trapped in abusive circumstances, and start taking action.

"Notice the red flags. Be aware of the abuse. Don't ignore it. Normalize speaking out."

Lucy currently lives in a single-home dwelling with her loving, patient, and supportive husband, her fourteen-year-old daughter, her six-year-old grandson—whom she and her husband legally adopted as their own—and their two family dogs: Tyson and Mia.

To my best loved friend
Jenni,

At the lowest point in my life when I thought I could go no further, you lifted me up and helped me to develope a backbone. You never let me feel sorry for myself and always let me know I was worth love and compassion. Thank you for living my Chin.
I'll love you forever and ever.

Your friend

Lucy L. Henson
4/28/2023

CPSIA information can be obtained
at www.ICGtesting.com
Printed in the USA
BVHW042155270922
648161BV00006B/163